*For stock-car fans loving motorsport
mystery and romance.*

Darlington dawn.

Vander Ploeg, Fred, & Nelson Miller.

Motor Racing Productions, LLC – May 2024

1527 Pineridge Drive
Grand Haven, MI 49417
USA

ISBN-13: 979-8-89292-857-1

All Rights Reserved
© 2024 Motor Racing Productions, LLC

1

Lane toyed with his cellphone, looking at it irritably.

"What's up, Babe?" Elena asked from across the motor home.

Elena knew Lane would be fidgety on the eve of his first Cup points race for his dad's old team. But Elena didn't expect a cellphone, of all things, to distract Lane.

"Nothing," Lane replied, trying to shake off the cellphone's distraction.

Elena shrugged, adopting her own irritable look at Lane's refusal.

Noticing Elena's irritation, and not wanting its more-serious distraction to weigh on him during the next day's Denton 500 season-opening race, Lane confessed.

"This thing's suddenly showing me ads for treatments for a medical condition no one but the stock-car association knows I have," Lane admitted.

When Lane had submitted to the exhaustive medical examinations and testing that the stock-car association administers before issuing a racing license, Lane had indeed discovered that he had an inherited medical condition that someday, likely in his old age, might need treatment. But the test results had properly remained confidential for the three years since then. No one but

Lane, his dad Blake, and his mom Diana knew. And now Elena.

Elena considered Lane's revelation for a moment. She could see that Lane wasn't concerned about the medical condition and instead only its apparent disclosure. So ignoring the medical condition, which she rightly assumed wasn't particularly consequential, Elena instead addressed Lane's irritating concern.

"They've gotten your medical records," Elena said bluntly.

"Who's *they*?" Lane said with increasing irritation.

"Whoever the stock-car association is using for data services," Elena replied, unmoved by Lane's irritation but with a hint of annoyance at Lane's naivete.

Elena shook her head in disbelief that Lane didn't see the lengths to which some tech companies go to promote their business, notwithstanding the legal, contractual, and privacy rights of others.

"How could that be possible?" Lane shot back.

But even as Lane said so, he realized that Elena was probably right. Lane knew that the stock-car association had just entered a new data-services agreement beginning that year. The new agreement had required all the race teams to conform their technology systems to the new provider's requirements. The new provider had access to everything from communications, finances, marketing, and administration right down to practice simulator data and the terabytes of on-track data the race cars produce.

"Ask your sister," Elena said nonchalantly in response to Lane's naive question. Elena could see that Lane already knew what had happened. The new tech provider had probably mined the medical, employment, financial, and other records of every stock-car association and team employee. Indeed, it had probably mined the data on millions of race fans. Elena knew that Lane was just trying to save face.

Elena had referred to Lane's younger sister Dani. Elena knew Dani was in tech. Elena didn't know anything about tech. But having accompanied her father Raoul on his nefarious business travels for so many years, Elena knew the power that technology can place in the hands of those who have access to it. Elena's father was in custody awaiting trial on international money-laundering charges.

Lane tossed his cellphone onto the seat next to him. Wanting to change the subject, or perhaps wanting to regain his standing at Elena's expense, he asked, "Heard anything on your father's trial date?"

Elena bristled. Lane realized the mistake he'd made. Indeed, he sensed for a moment the bitter spirit that had caused his subtle dig at his beloved Elena. He knew they'd be arguing in another minute.

Lane and Elena had progressed in their relationship in the three months since the Cup season had ended. They hadn't argued. They weren't living together, as they had initially. But they were dating. And they were learning to see more of the character, depth, and interests of one another. They were learning how to care for one another in the new life each was leading.

Elena was working for Lane's Aunt Marla, running the race team Marla and her husband Rob owned with Lane's parents Blake and Diana. That race team fielded cars in the series below the top-level Cup series.

Lane had taken his dad Blake's Cup series seat on a leading Cup team, after Blake had retired at the end of the prior year. Blake had won the Cup championship. Lane, who hadn't qualified for the Cup championship in his rookie year in the Cup series, had won the Cup championship race right in front of his dad. Lane's first Cup win had cemented his place as his famous dad's heir apparent.

Their new lives were a lot for Lane and Elena to handle. And then, Elena had to recover from her father's arrest. Elena had played a key role in Raoul's arrest, as had Lane, his Uncle Rob, and others in their stock-car association circle.

Trying to think of something to say to recover from his gaffe, Lane said to Elena as tenderly as he could manage, "You must still feel relieved to be free from his grip."

Elena nodded involuntarily, without looking at Lane. The argument Lane's comment had stirred still lingered in the luxurious motorhome's close interior. Elena was glad, but she didn't feel like showing it.

Instead, Elena motioned with her chin toward the cellphone on the seat next to Lane, saying, "At least I could see my captor."

Lane gave Elena a curious look but then got it. He nodded. Elena was right once again. Lane was captive to whomever or whatever controlled the screens into which he, his competitors, and the rest of the world spent increasing amounts of time staring.

"I'll ask Dani about it," Lane replied, glad to defuse the argument that had threatened to burden them both right before Lane's first big Cup points race with his new team.

Elena nodded. She was glad, too, that they had found a way to dissolve their tension. They were indeed learning to care for one another, although they had a long way to go.

Elena rose, moved to Lane's seat, and leaned down to give him a kiss, but a knock on the motorhome door interrupted them. With a look of disappointment, Elena moved to the door to swing it open. Marla stood outside. Rob was behind her.

"Ready, Sweetheart?" Marla asked, looking up into the motorhome at Elena.

Elena nodded. She turned quickly back to Lane, gave him a rich kiss and bright smile, grabbed her bag, and headed out to join Marla. Rob watched Marla and Elena go and then headed into the motorhome to join Lane.

Evenings before a race are sensitive times for Cup series drivers. They need rest. They need a clear head. And they don't need stress or distraction. Routines help drivers get what they need while avoiding what they don't need.

In a new Cup car on a new team, Lane needed a new routine. Rob knew so. That's why he stopped by Lane's motorhome.

"Want to walk down to your garage?" Rob asked.

"Just got back. Everything's all set," Lane replied. He added with a smile at Rob, "They told me to get out of there."

Rob smiled back. He was glad to see Lane able to smile about something. He knew the tremendous pressure Lane might feel taking his dad's Cup seat for a leading team, while immediately facing the biggest race of the year.

"Mind if I sit for a bit?" Rob asked, motioning toward the seat that Elena had just vacated.

"Please do," Lane replied lightly, sensing that Rob's visit might be the start of a helpful new routine.

Lane liked Rob. He also trusted Rob, especially after the expert way Rob had handled Raoul's challenging arrest. Rob was a military special-operations veteran, one of the qualifications he held for the security work he did for the stock-car association.

As Rob took his seat, Lane realized how much he appreciated and needed Rob. If Lane was going to succeed his dad Blake as a champion Cup driver, Lane was going to need Rob.

Blake, of course, would remain by Lane's side for whatever Lane needed. But Lane and Blake had kept a respectful distance from one another as Lane grew up. Blake hadn't wanted to pressure Lane to drive. And Lane hadn't wanted anyone, especially himself, to feel that Lane was riding his dad's coattails into a Cup ride. Lane had thus been closer to his Uncle Rob than to his dad.

Lane glanced at his cellphone on the seat next to him. As he did so, he remembered his annoyance over the advertisement. He decided to tell Rob. He finished by asking Rob if the new tech provider might have harvested medical data.

"Could be," Rob replied, nodding. He thought for a moment before continuing, "I don't want to say anything to distract you from tomorrow's race. Just trust that I'm already on it. You're not the first to notice.

And in the meantime, tell me the moment you see anything else suspicious."

Lane nodded, raising his eyebrows. Then he shook his head, as if to cast off a spell.

"Look," Lane said to Rob, "I'm not really that worried about it. Everyone's doing it. They're just trying to sell products."

Rob looked at Lane, thinking how much or how little he should share. Lane looked so young. Rob would have told his dad Blake everything. But Rob wasn't sure Lane was ready to handle what his dad would have handled, with courage and aplomb. Better to wait, Rob decided. Lane had a big day tomorrow, his first race in his dad's old seat, with his new team.

A knock on the motorhome door interrupted Rob's musing. Lane rose, stepped to the door, and swung it open.

"Hey ya!" Billy the spotter said to Lane from outside the motorhome, "Want some company?"

"Join the party," Lane said with a wry smile.

Billy had the same thought as Rob: Lane needed a new pre-race routine. What better than spending an hour or two the evening before, shooting the breeze with your spotter?

Billy had spotted for Lane's dad Blake for years and years. Billy's loose humor and relaxed personality had been the perfect balance for Blake's serious, introverted nature.

Billy also had a sixth sense for what was going on in a race, earned from years of immersion in the sport. Billy had turned spotting from a science of precise observation and instant communication into an art form, perhaps even a philosophy. Billy didn't just look at a *race* as a spotter must, telling his driver exactly what was happening on the track around his driver. Billy looked at the *world* as a spotter, always on the lookout, always seeing things just before they happened, and always trying to give fair warning.

Billy mounted the motorhome steps with a groan, saying, "You need a motorhome with fewer steps."

"You win us the race tomorrow," Lane quipped back with a smile, "And I'll have this thing made into a lowrider."

"The world's first lowriding motorhome!" Billy cheered as he plopped into a seat with another groan. Nodding to Rob, Billy grunted, "Good to see you, 007. What's happening in the cold war?"

Rob chuckled, replying, "Same old. Still on the wall, looking for the next demon."

"Oh, I'm sure the next demon's already at work," Billy replied with his own chuckle, adding, "Those things don't rest."

A beep went off somewhere in the motorhome. Lane, Rob, and Billy all reached for their cellphones. Billy's device was the offender. After pulling it from his pocket, he thumbed and tapped through its screens until satisfied that he had momentarily tamed the device's demon.

"Darn thing knows more about me than my wife does," Billy growled with an irritated look. He added, "The thing somehow knows I had a high school football injury. Even I'd forgotten."

Lane looked at Rob. Rob subtly shook his head, indicating to Lane to keep their discussion between them. Lane nodded.

"Any last instructions for tomorrow, Big Guy?" Billy asked Lane.

Lane looked down at his hands, shaking his head. Billy sensed the weight Lane was feeling.

Lane had worked hard over the offseason, since the Cup championship race in early November. Nearly everyone on Lane's new team had taken substantial time off, many of them right through to the first of the year. They'd earned it, after nine solid months of racing, across three dozen race weekends, at more than two dozen race tracks coast to coast. Lane, though, had kept checking in at his new race team's headquarters, trying to get a head start.

Billy had been the one who'd anticipated Lane's eagerness. Billy had needed the break as much as anyone else on the team. But Billy, as much as anyone else, lived and breathed the sport. And Billy had that spotter's sixth sense, even about the team's new driver Lane. Billy had heard that Lane was at the race facility and had immediately come in to take Lane under his wing. Billy had then quietly navigated team vacation schedules and politics to ensure that Lane got the head start Lane wanted and needed.

Billy hadn't been concerned about his spotter's job. He knew Lane would have a key role in selecting his own spotter. Billy would have been fine with spotting for someone else or taking another role for the team. He'd even have been fine with retiring, after a long and rewarding career spotting for Lane's Cup champion dad.

But Billy's sixth sense that Lane would need and welcome Billy's tutelage led to Lane confirming that Billy would remain the spotter for Lane's dad's old car.

Billy looked at Lane again, thinking how young, innocent, and vulnerable he looked. Strange to think of a race car driver in that way, Billy mused. They exhibit such incredible courage climbing into those two-hundred-mile-an-hour contraptions. But here it was again, a young and extraordinarily skilled race car driver at the gorgeous dawn of what just might be a spectacular career. The thought finally led Billy to say what he'd been searching to grasp.

"Hey, Bud," Billy said quietly to Lane. Lane looked up at Billy.

"I'm proud to be a part of this moment," Billy said, more seriously than Lane had ever seen Billy. Billy paused before resuming, "And I want to thank you for letting me be a part of it."

Lane quickly looked down again, shaking his head. He wiped away the tears forming against his will in his eyes. He'd been so cool and collected all week, indeed all offseason. Why would the emotion come now?

But Billy knew what Lane had been holding in all offseason, that bundle of fears and insecurities that every young driver feels, but tries to cover up with braggadocio, when joining the elite club of Cup drivers.

Lane had raced the prior Cup season. Lane wasn't a rookie. But Lane had raced the prior Cup season in a Cup seat that his dad and aunt had borrowed for the season. Although Lane had earned that seat through his success in the stock-car association's lower levels, Lane had nonetheless raced in his own mind, and in the minds of many fans, on his dad's coattails. But now, Lane was about to race on his own, for one of the sport's great race teams. And he could not help but feel the moment's weight.

Billy had come to the motorhome that evening on a mission to make one last try at letting Lane unload that weight. And Billy's kind words had done the trick.

Lane sobbed, without even knowing why.

Billy and Rob let him do so, without a word or gesture. Women would have hugged it out. Men in another field might have done so, too. But the race driver's code and custom dictated exactly what Billy and Rob did, sitting respectfully, letting Lane wonder on his own at the mystery of the mind, body, and emotions.

Lane soon composed himself. Billy and Rob ignored him, making small talk between themselves. But their small talk wasn't aimless. In fact, they both knew that they were turning their conversation toward things that would feed Lane's aching soul, in the way that dads talk among themselves knowing that their children are listening. Billy and Rob could each remember wisdom their fathers had imparted to them, not speaking to them but speaking to a peer while in their presence. One learns more from overhearing a conversation than listening to a lecture.

"So, another year of spotting?" Rob asked Billy.

"Yeah," Billy replied, looking down at his hands while adding, "The thing definitely has its grip."

Rob nodded, replying, "It's good to investigate what attracts your attention, huh?"

Billy looked up at Rob with a smile, knowing that Rob had just turned the conversation philosophical. Billy liked that about Rob. Rob had a way of putting common sense originally. After a pause, Rob continued.

"It's like Moses turning aside to consider the burning bush. In doing so, he received a vision of the promised land."

Rob paused again. Billy's smile broadened, urging Rob on. Lane had set his cellphone aside to listen. Rob pretended to ignore Lane, speaking to Billy instead.

"It's not the same as pursuing distractions," Rob said with a glance at Lane's cellphone on the seat beside Lane. Rob continued, "It's putting your faith in what beckons you from afar, from the mountaintop. That's what leads you forward and upward through a healthy, meaningful, non-anxious life."

Billy chuckled, saying, "Now that's a mindful."

"Yes, I suppose so," Rob replied with a glance down. But he soon resumed, saying, "Pursuing the things that attract your best attention is like listening to your conscience's call, that thing that is so hard to hear in a distracted world."

Billy nodded, saying, "Better take responsibility, or someone else will take it and use it against you."

Rob smiled, nodding. He added, "Pursue the ultimate at the top, because it's already pursuing you. The meaning with which the creator imbued our world invites transcendence, pointing to the highest unifying person and principle. A life of meaning is joining with others in pointing upward to the highest."

Billy laughed, saying, "Well put, Philosopher." Turning to Lane, Billy added, "Glad to have you pointing up with us.

Darlington Dawn

The three laughed together.

2

"I'd call it a disaster," Lane admitted disconsolately, referring to his Denton 500 results. He turned his half-empty coffee mug back and forth on the table in front of him, fidgeting away his unhappy, restless energy.

Lane had met Elena at Rob and Marla's house back in Charlotte Tuesday evening, after the season-opening Cup points race in Denton, one that had gone poorly for Lane. Dani had joined them.

Tuesday evenings during the racing season were family time. They were that one moment in the week when everyone had recovered sufficiently from the prior race but not yet fully immersed themselves in preparations for the next race.

To Rob and Marla, it felt strange not to have Blake and Diana there. They had started the Tuesday-evening tradition way back when Blake and Diana were first dating. But now, with Blake's retirement, he and Diana had said they had other plans, at least this first Tuesday evening of the new season. Rob and Marla knew they had manufactured those plans. Lane didn't need mom and dad reliving every wrinkle of the new racing season.

Elena, sitting next to Lane at the kitchen table, put her hand on Lane's hand, stilling his fidgeting. Lane looked up at her with a smile.

Lane's feelings for Elena had continued to change over the off season. When they first met and started dating, Lane had fallen passionately in love with Elena's mysteriousness. That mystery, though, had nearly destroyed both of them. Rob had helped extricate them from Raoul's international money- laundering enterprise. Elena's mystery had turned out to be dark, alluring in the worst possible way.

Stripped of that horrible darkness, Elena appeared to Lane to have a new light. Lane and Elena had each wondered whether Elena's rescue from her father's grip and gradual recovery would so fundamentally change their relationship as to end it. Elena had moved out of Lane's condominium and in with Rob and Marla to give Lane and Elena a chance to start over—if they wished to do so.

The move had been wise. Time would tell whether it would save their relationship.

Over the off season, Lane had spent time thinking of how couples came together. Initially, he had thought that few did so in rescue of one or the other. Gradually, though, he had realized that all couples did so. Every parting from one's family of origin is a rescue, even if not nearly as dramatic as escaping an abusive international money-laundering mastermind.

Over the off season, Lane had drawn from conversations with Rob, Billy, his team owner, and others that every life has a vision, the vision of its creator. Visions, though, aren't building on one's family inheritance. Visions move one to one's own ground, to till richly with another of her own peculiar origins. Visions involve disruptive regeneration. Family traditions stabilize, providing critical continuity. But they also ossify, choking out new life.

New life always arises from a marriage of heaven and earth, of the masculine with the feminine, the creator with his creation.

Lane put his other hand atop Elena's hand, as he continued to look at her with a smile. Elena put her free hand atop his, their hands now joined. She smiled.

Elena's rare smile flooded Lane once again with hope for their relationship. Elena had never smiled when Lane first met her. For months, he hadn't even known she was capable of smiling, thinking maybe it was a cultural thing. But unwinding Raoul's grip had freed the suppressed smile from within Elena. Everyone has a smile. Despair just suppresses some smiles deep within.

Dani let the sweet moment pass between her brother and Elena. Finally, she spoke.

"Races are one winner followed by three dozen disasters," Dani quipped. She let the smiles and chuckles subside before adding, "The question is always what to learn from the disaster."

Lane liked Dani's logical character, so like their dad Blake. Lane had their mother Diana's emotion, Dani their dad's logic. Dani's words unleashed a torrent of frustration from Lane.

"It seemed like nothing went right from the start," Lane began before listing, "The radio didn't work right, the tire pressures were off from the gun data, the pit-lane-speed dash lights failed, the simulator data threw us way off on setup. It was like we were racing with a bad connection."

"Sounds like the tech demons got you," Dani summarized.

Lane paused. Until his outburst, he hadn't seen how so many of his race team's problems had a common source in their data failings. And Lane hadn't thought of his cellphone, his medical condition, and his conversation with Rob about the sport's new data provider. Lane shot a glance at Rob who, catching Lane's glance, raised his eyebrows.

"You haven't seen anything yet," Elena said quietly in her old, low, monotone voice. Looking up to see the surprise on the others' faces, she added, "I'm sorry."

"No, no," Marla said quickly to Elena, "That's alright. You've sensed something and shared it with us. Never hesitate to do so."

Lane shot another glance at Rob who gently shook his head. Rob wasn't ready to get into a full discussion of what a tech provider might do with the sport's data in the worst case. Time would tell whether that discussion would be necessary.

Dani noticed Lane's glance at Rob and Rob's quiet signal back. She quickly resolved to speak with Lane later but to respect Rob's wishes.

"Well," Dani piped up, speaking to Lane, "I'm sure you've already been hard at work setting things right for the next race."

Lane smiled at Dani, nodding. He, too, wanted to move on quickly, and so he replied, "Some good tracks are coming up, too."

The evening's family business wasn't over, though.

"You've got something new on your own plate," Marla said to Dani with a smile and wink.

Dani blushed.

Dani had enlisted Marla to help her with something she'd been wanting to share with Lane. And it wasn't going to be easy.

Lane looked at Marla, then looked at Dani, and then back to Marla. He sensed something was coming he might not like.

Seeing Dani's silent blush, Marla decided she needed to break the ice. But Rob unintentionally beat her to it.

"Let me guess," Rob interjected with a laugh, "Dani's got a hot new date."

Dani shot a look of defiance toward Rob. Rob's mouth dropped open.

"Did I just put my foot in my mouth?" Rob asked.

Marla nodded, saying wryly, "It wouldn't be the first time."

"Indeed," Rob replied sheepishly, "I broke a cardinal rule: never shall a man speak of such things in the presence of interested women."

Lane, watching Dani squirm, was growing impatient with the small talk. Looking at Dani, he asked as kindly and gently as he could, "Who's the lucky guy?"

Dani shook her head without looking up. Things were going about as poorly as she could have imagined. She felt as if she were in a swamped dinghy adrift on a turbulent sea. Marla knew it was her role to try bailing Dani out.

"Well," Marla replied slyly to Lane, "Let's just say it's someone you know."

Lane sat back in his seat. His mind ran quickly through a catalog of eligible young men he knew, roughly his own age. As he did so, he was reading Marla's expression. Then it dawned on him.

Lane's first reaction was a small shake of his head to himself. If it was true that Dani was dating his new teammate Darnell, then Lane's whole world had just skipped a beat from a seismic shift in relationships.

Dani looked up at Lane. Reading his countenance like only a sister could, Dani knew that Lane knew who her boyfriend was. Lane looked back at Dani. Dani tipped her head lightly, shrugged, and gave Lane her best Bambi eyes. Lane shook his head but smiled. Dani smiled back.

"Just wait until I get my hands on him," Lane said jokingly.

Lane spent much of the next day on the simulator at the race facility, tuning up for the next weekend's race. The simulator had a dual role. It reminded the drivers of the track's layout, as they rehearsed lap after virtual lap, turning calculated actions into the autonomic responses on which they would depend throughout the race. Racing leaves little time for thinking. What a driver does without thinking can count for more.

But the simulator also helped the team's race engineer and crew chief test dozens or even hundreds of car setups against their driver's preferences and techniques. The simulator let the team install a setup to hone in practice and perfect in qualifying, for the start of the race. The pit crew would then adjust what they could on the fly throughout the race.

The setup for the prior weekend's Denton 500, though, had been so poor that the crew chief and race engineer were sure something was wrong with the simulator. Yet the simulator's technicians had checked it out thoroughly on Monday and Tuesday, finding no problems. They suggested instead to check with the sport's new data provider. Its new connections might be scrambling the data.

The race engineer entered the simulator room behind Lane, giving him a tap on the shoulder.

"Take a break," the race engineer said to Lane after Lane had looked up and pulled his headset back from one ear.

The engineer gave a jerk of his head toward a figure who had entered the room behind him. The engineer explained to Lane, "The tech company's going over some things."

The engineer turned and left. Lane climbed from the simulator. He stood looking at the nondescript figure already poking around at the simulator's connections.

Lane had the brief thought of greeting the figure. But he saw no opportunity. Indeed, from the figure's dark glasses, close-cropped hair, loose gray uniform, and silently officious manner, Lane couldn't even tell whether the figure was a man or woman. Ignoring Lane, the figure kept looking at an electronic device with a tiny screen held in one hand, while fiddling with connections with the free hand.

Irritated at the figure's officiousness, Lane decided to try a greeting anyway.

"Hi," he said while offering a handshake, "I'm Lane."

The figure didn't acknowledge Lane. Affronted, Lane added pointedly, "You're...?"

"From the directorate," the figure replied, completing Lane's sentence without looking at Lane or acknowledging Lane's extended hand. The figure continued its investigations.

Lane shrugged, gave a dismissive wave of his hand toward the busy figure, and turned to walk out.

"The algorithm isn't going to like that," the figure said.

Lane stopped, turned back, and looked again at the figure. The figure had paused its investigations to look straight at Lane. Its dark glasses and stoic expression concealed any emotion. Lane shook his head as if to make sure he wasn't dreaming.

"Isn't going to like what?" Lane finally asked, adding, "And what algorithm?"

The figure stared blankly back at Lane for another moment before turning away to resume its investigations. Lane shrugged again and turned again to go.

"I'd be careful if I were you," the figure said as Lane stepped toward the door.

Lane stopped again to look back at the figure. But the figure was busy fiddling with connections while looking at the tiny screen of its handheld device. Lane wondered if he had really heard the warning or had made it up.

Shaking his head once again, Lane turned and left the room.

Lane quickly put the encounter out of mind. He had to do so. He had the next race for which to prepare. And he wanted that race to go much better than the Denton 500 had gone.

By day's end, Lane's crew chief and race engineer felt they had what they needed from Lane's simulator work for a strong setup. Lane felt race ready, too.

By day's end, Lane had also navigated an issue that could prove just as important on and off the track as an initial car setup. Lane had crossed paths with his teammate, Dani's new boyfriend, Darnell.

Darnell had joined the organization the year before. Lane was the race team rookie, in only his second Cup series year. Darnell was also in his second Cup year. But while Lane had raced on a new one-car, one-season Cup team the prior year, Darnell had raced alongside Lane's dad Blake on that organization's four-car team. Lane and Darnell were now teammates and second-year Cup drivers. But Darnell already had a year under his belt on their current four-car team.

Lane thus already had a curious relationship with Darnell. Lane didn't look up to Darnell as a senior driver. But Lane had to look up to Darnell as his slight senior, even if only by one year, on their current race team. Lane was the newcomer. Darnell was not.

Now that everyone was learning that Darnell and Lane's sister were dating, the good-natured teasing of both Lane and Darnell had already begun.

"Better watch out," someone in the facility's lunchroom said, "Here comes big brother."

Darnell looked up from his sandwich to see Lane entering the lunchroom. Lane grabbed a snack from the counter, walked over, and sat down at the table with Darnell. Lane greeted everyone at the table without acknowledging Darnell. The others snickered. Darnell gave them a mock glare.

"So how's everyone feeling about the coming race?" Lane asked, again studiously ignoring Darnell.

The others snickered again, sensing that this moment was going to be every bit as fun as they'd anticipated. Lane was clearly playing along.

No one answered Lane, but he continued anyway, saying, "Yeah, good, then. I'm feeling the same way."

The others snickered again. Lane turned to Darnell.

"How's your dog doing, buddy?" Lane asked him.

Everyone knew Darnell was a dog lover. He'd just gotten a new hunting dog. The others snickered again. Darnell smiled, deciding he'd play along.

"Doing great," Darnell replied, "Doing great. Do you know anyone who can care for him while we're away?"

"Like a house sitter?" Lane asked. When Darnell nodded, Lane added, "I'll have to ask Dani. She might know someone."

The others all laughed. One of them said, "Yeah, Darnell. Let Lane ask Dani for you. You know, Lane's sister."

The others all laughed again. Laughing with them, Lane rose to go, saying, "I'll get back to you on that, Bud. See you later."

The others laughed again, clapping Darnell on the back as they did so.

Lane was looking forward to the next race. Racers who lose generally do. Redemption is only one race away for every losing driver. With a Cup field of around forty drivers, and only thirty-six races in the whole season, a single win can make a year for a young driver or a driver with a small team.

Lane, like nearly every other driver, could quickly put a losing race behind him. Lane didn't even feel substantial pressure yet to win. It was so early in the season that teams, sponsors, crews, fans, and drivers were generally willing to let things begin to sort themselves out.

Lane just wanted his team's dial pointing up. He just wanted out of the next race the sense that things were on the mend and improving. He wanted that elusive thing everyone calls *momentum*, but no one has ever seen, held, defined, bottled, or sold.

Lane just didn't want to start the new season with his new team in his dad's old seat, with a long losing streak, making it look like Lane wasn't up to the challenge. Lane didn't want the questions, the doubt, the soul searching, the agony that drivers feel when they can sense sponsors pulling back, crew members whispering doubts, and team owners holding secret meetings.

As he plumbed his own soul, Lane realized he wanted to impress Elena. Lane wanted Elena to see him winning races and to get to share in the excitement and celebration of it. Lane wanted to lift Elena up out of a sort of doldrums or even despair that she must feel over her new but undefined place in the world. Lane wanted to become for Elena what his dad Blake had been for his mom Diana.

The trouble was, Lane wasn't going to have that early success. Lane's struggles were going to continue. Disaster was going to follow disaster until Lane, Elena, Dani, and Rob faced the demon they all knew was lurking.

In pursuing a racing career, Lane had assumed in spades a challenge we all face. That challenge is to register and represent reality through our technology, including both language and tools. We all face that challenge. Race car drivers just do so publicly, measured every weekend by a different race track. Race tracks may be artificial, but real limits bound them. Reality imposes itself on the track.

The demon with which Lane wrestled, in meeting that challenge to register and respect reality, is not to let technology interpose itself. We all wrestle with that challenge. We all use technology. We must not let technology use us.

We must not make an idol of technology, for then technology will lead us away from the good inherent in reality. Reality blesses, while virtual reality carries technology's curse. The biblical God feeds, while the pagan gods consume. Reality is good, beautiful, and nurturing while also dangerous. Technology increases power but lures us into situations of danger when the technology fails. Progress is thus also regress.

Lane would soon need to remove the mediating technologies to see reality itself.

3

"What are they doing in the race garage?" Lane complained to his crew chief. Lane had just joined his team at the Las Vegas Motor Speedway pit garage. It was now the third Cup points race of the season.

The crew chief shrugged, saying, "Another inspection, I guess."

Lane watched as several android-like figures, with identical gray uniforms, dark sunglasses, and close-cropped hair, moved around the car and equipment. They each held the same device that the figure who had examined the simulator had held. They each likewise stared at their device's tiny screen.

The mechanics, crew chief, and race engineer stood back and watched as the figures moved officiously about, poking and prodding at car, equipment, and connections.

Recalling his irritation over the simulator inspection, Lane stepped forward into the path of one of the android figures.

"Hi, I'm Lane," he said, sticking his hand out for a handshake.

The figure looked briefly up at Lane from his device, shook his head, and stepped around Lane to continue with his inspections.

"I wouldn't do that if I were you," the crew chief observed dryly, "They don't like interruptions."

"Well, neither do I," Lane said.

Lane turned from the crew chief to announce across the race garage, "The inspection's over. Come back in two hours. We've got work to do."

The figures stopped. The figure nearest Lane looked up at him and then looked back at his device. Reading the device's tiny screen, the figure announced to the others, "The algorithm says to continue."

The figures all resumed their inspection, ignoring Lane.

Lane stepped in front of the figure who had made the countermanding announcement. The crew chief tried to stop Lane but was too late. The figure looked up at Lane. Lane looked back at the figure. The figure tapped its hand-held device. Within seconds, a taller figure appeared at the open race-garage door.

"What have we here?" the tall figure asked in a grand voice, adding with a hint of humor, "Getting to know one another?"

Lane turned to regard the tall figure who stepped forward with an outstretched hand.

"Doyle," the tall figure introduced himself to Lane as they shook hands, adding his title, "Council chief."

"I'm Lane," Lane replied.

"I know," Doyle replied with a dismissive wave of his hand. To be sure Lane got the point, Doyle added with a sly smile, "No need to introduce anyone else, either. I know not just their names but also their ages, birthdates, and favorite desserts, too."

"And medical histories," Lane corrected Doyle with a glare.

Doyle raised his eyebrows, replying coolly, "Perhaps so, perhaps so."

Lane and Doyle regarded one another silently. Each knew in that instant that they had met a worthy adversary. Each also knew in that instant that the other would in some sense hold their fate. But each also knew that the resolution of their adversarial stances would only come in time and that the time was not now.

Doyle was the first to speak. In as condescending a fashion as Lane had ever heard another speak, Doyle said slowly, "My minions must be disturbing your little race preparations, no?"

Lane felt Doyle laughing derisively as he said so. But Lane knew that he was only reading Doyle's spirit.

Lane nodded once in response, silently, without removing his firm stare into Doyle's cold eyes.

"Come on, then," Doyle said to the figures, adding a snap of his fingers but without looking away from Lane.

The figures all snapped to attention, swiftly melting out of the race garage.

"There," Doyle said as the last figure left, still staring back at Lane. He added, "Does that help?"

Lane turned from Doyle to his crew chief, saying quietly, "Let's get back to work."

The crew chief, race engineer, and mechanics slowly resumed their activity around the car and at the counter in the back of the race garage, each with watchful eyes toward Lane and Doyle. Lane watched his crew resume their work. Doyle stood watching Lane.

Finally, Doyle turned and walked out the open garage door. Lane watched him go, suspecting that he wouldn't go quietly. And indeed, Doyle stopped just beyond the door, turned back to Lane, and asked, "Do you really think that was such a good idea?"

Lane understood Doyle's threat. He just didn't know how far Doyle's council might take it. Rather than respond, Lane turned to address his crew chief. When a moment later Lane glanced back where Doyle had stood, he was gone.

Lane shook his head, trying to clear it of the episode. His race team had so much on which to work.

The season's second Cup points race had produced disappointing results for Lane much like the Denton 500. The whole team had just seemed off from the race week's start to the finish of the race itself. The simulator work hadn't produced a helpful setup. The car had unloaded slow. Practice had, if anything, made it slower. The car qualified poorly, closer to the back than the front. Adjustments the team made during the race didn't seem to help.

Lane had driven the second race with the same confidence he drove every other race. He expected to at least gain track position throughout the race, if not to win the race. Billy had done his part from the rooftop spotter's stand, guiding Lane expertly through the race.

But as hard and smart as everyone tried, nothing clicked. Lane gained no track position. He even lost a few spots. Lane finished the race, which was a small victory in itself. But he finished off the lead lap.

For Lane, the hard part of processing his second race was that it didn't point to any solution. Nothing stood out as needing fixing. Lane almost would have preferred to crash or blow an engine because of a failed part, or have a competitor ruin his race. Then, at least the team would have had something to which to point, to explain the disappointing results.

Lane and his crew chief had discussed their conundrum at length, without coming up with any clear direction for the team. That's why the garage time seemed extra important. Without anything specific on which to work, the team needed to discover something to move them forward. They needed to find an issue, discover a boundary, create an edge.

The team worked late into the night, looking for that edge. With qualifying the next day, they needed it.

Elena and Dani met Lane at his motorhome the next morning. Elena had been traveling to the race tracks with Marla, as Marla directed Blake's race team in the stock-car association's next lower level. Dani didn't usually travel to races, but a certain new boyfriend had invited her to Las Vegas.

After a little small talk over their long travels and local diversions, Lane shared his encounter with the tech council and its head Doyle the evening before.

"I suppose they're just doing their due diligence on collecting accurate race data," Lane concluded, adding, "Maybe I shouldn't have given them such a hard time."

"They don't just collect data," Elena corrected Lane. She added, "They analyze, use, broker, and sell it."

"I know they collect and share with the media and other teams the car and equipment data, even on small things like the air-pressure spikes on the guns we use to change tires at every pit stop," Lane acknowledged.

"That's not what I said," Elena corrected Lane again. She added, "I said they analyze and use it, not just collect and share it. And then they broker and sell it."

"How do you know?" Lane asked Elena, more sharply than he had intended.

"It's possible and profitable, and no one's stopping them," Elena replied jadedly, ignoring Lane's sharp and challenging tone.

"Use it how?" Lane asked doubtingly, adding, "And sell it to whom?"

Elena turned to Dani, asking, "If you had zero scruples, how would you use and sell race car data for the greatest profit and control?"

Dani looked at Lane. Lane shrugged. So Dani answered, "Well, I could analyze car performance and sell it to bettors."

Elena shrugged, saying, "Maybe. But with this level of access and control, you could do a lot better." Elena paused before correcting herself, saying, "I mean, a lot worse."

Dani hesitated. She looked at Lane again. Lane raised his eyebrows, shook his head, and shrugged. So Dani answered, "You mean manipulate data to fix races."

Elena nodded. Lane's jaw dropped open. Seeing so, Elena added defiantly, "But you could do even better. Meaning do even worse."

Dani looked back and forth from Elena to Lane. She hadn't meant to get in the middle of an argument. But she was in now, and she knew what Elena meant, so she said it.

"You mean directly controlling race outcomes."

"That's right," Elena said matter of factly.

Lane shook his head back and forth, as if Elena's suggestion was impossible. Noticing Lane's disbelief, Elena asked Dani, "That wouldn't be hard, would it?"

Dani thought for a moment before replying, "Well, if they're pulling data from the cars and equipment, they could push data, too. And they could push whatever data they wished, improving or corrupting car and equipment performance."

Elena shrugged, saying, "Yes, not hard. But they could just as well broker driver, team member, or even fan data to the IRS, Department of Homeland Security, credit-card companies, and scammers worldwide."

"But why?" Lane finally asked, no longer willing to challenge the premise.

"If you don't have scruples, then why not?" Elena asked.

"But why should I assume that they're dishonest?" Lane asked.

"I didn't suggest you assume anything," Elena replied. She calmly explained, "I was just going by what you yourself said. You've had only two encounters with them, and they threatened you both times. Take them at face value. They demand control. And they've already told you that they are willing to use it against you, simply for questioning their actions. That's not simple dishonesty. That's outright evil."

Lane sat stunned, mouth agape. He hadn't liked the council's intrusions. He hadn't liked the soulless attitudes of their workers or the imperiousness of their leader Doyle. But did he really need to assume their actions to be evil?

"Let me speak with Rob about it," Dani said.

Dani could see that Lane needed a truce. Qualifying was coming up. Lane needed to think about racing, not tech conspiracies. Unless, of course, the two were connected. Then, Lane needed to think about both. Dani made a mental note to play out the worst-case scenarios with Rob.

Lane, though, had one last question. After a respectful pause to let both Elena and Dani know that the truce was on, Lane asked, "What's this algorithm they keep mentioning?"

Dani took a quick glance at Elena who looked bored.

"Let's leave that one for Rob," Dani suggested.

Lane nodded while looking at his watch and saying, "Right. I've got to get to the garage."

The three rose together. Lane stepped to Elena and gave her a hug, whispering *thank you* in her ear as he did so.

Elena smiled at Lane, that rare warm smile that was becoming less rare and more familiar. Lane smiled back. Lane then turned to Dani.

"Tell Darnell I'm beating him in qualifying," Lane said with a mock note of seriousness.

Dani laughed, saying, "I hope you do. He's riding a bit too high right now."

Dani was right. Darnell had done well at the prior weekend's race, better than anyone but his own team expected.

Lane did beat Darnell in qualifying at Las Vegas Motor Speedway that afternoon. But neither driver was pleased with the outcome. Both drivers qualified in the back half of the field.

That evening before the next day's big Cup race, Rob and Billy joined Lane in his motorhome, confirming the tradition they had started with Lane just two weeks earlier. Rob's depth and Billy's humor were proving to be exactly the right combination for Lane for the evening before the Cup race.

Race drivers generally have a bold and fearless side, the side that tells them to throw caution to the wind. Every ride in a two-hundred-mile-an-hour vehicle takes a wild side. But race drivers also have a reflective side. Wild rides, like hallucinogens, can open doors for reflection. As a spotter, Billy had the spirit of the wild ride. As a security director, Rob had the spirit of reflection.

Their sparse conversation soon turned to the subject Lane had broached earlier in the day with Elena and Dani. Lane shared with Rob his encounter with the council figures and its leader Doyle. Lane included in his account the second mention Lane had heard from the figures about the algorithm determining their actions.

"They don't really have a formula they follow, do they?" Lane asked Rob.

"In a broader sense, yes," Rob replied after a moment's reflection. He explained, "But it's better to think of the algorithm as a totalizing spirit than a formula or set of formulas."

Rob let his reply sink in. Billy, though, rolled his eyes at Lane, saying, "The only spirit I know is the one in those cans I brought with me."

Lane and Rob laughed. But Rob then resumed.

"Tech companies treat data as fungible, analyzable, subject to patterns, packaging, and control. To a degree, they have to do so. Hence their algorithms, which are just sets of problem-solving rules."

Rob paused again. Lane interjected, "Nothing wrong with that, is there?"

"No," Rob replied cautiously, while adding, "Not in itself. We all follow rules or heuristics. We couldn't get through a day without them."

Billy, who was only half-listening to the conversation, held his hands wide apart while interjecting, "My dad had a heuristic. It was about *yay* long. He'd pull it out of the closet and use it on me every time I did something wrong."

Lane and Rob both laughed. Lane then turned the conversation back to Rob's insight.

"So what's this *totalizing spirit*?" Lane asked Rob.

"Well," Rob replied, choosing his words carefully, "Tech companies derive power and profit from applying their algorithms, their problem-solving rules. And the bigger the company and greater the quantity of data, the more power and profit they can derive."

Rob paused again. Lane interjected, "But power and profit come from a lot of things."

Rob nodded, explaining, "That's where the totalizing spirit comes in. In other fields, power and profit may derive from transactions, service, beauty, fear, or any number of things. In the data field, though, power and profit arise from controlling and shaping, and ultimately constricting, the data flow. The spirit of data is a totalizing spirit, a *tyrannical* spirit."

Lane gave Rob a puzzled look. Rob smiled.

"Don't look so confused," Rob said with a chuckle, adding, "That tyrannical spirit is all around us. It's the spirit of the information age."

Lane shook his head. He reached for his cellphone on the seat beside him. Holding it up, he said to Rob, "What do you mean *tyrannical*? We're freer with these devices than ever before."

"Oh, really?" Rob replied with his eyebrows raised, adding, "Like freer to travel, despite the health passports that civilized nations worldwide impose? And freer to share our views, despite the banning, blocking, and canceling platforms impose? And freer to ply our trades, despite license revocations and job terminations for exploring a disfavored view? And freer to save and spend our money, despite government financial seizures and buying controls?"

Rob paused. Lane shrugged, saying only, "It feels like freedom."

Rob smiled. Nodding, he said, "Exactly so. Until you step ever so slightly out of your lane. And then you're not free at all."

"Maybe," Lane replied, adding, "But I still don't get the tyranny thing."

Rob thought for another moment before concluding, "The totalizing spirit must destroy the anomaly, especially anything or anyone appearing to transcend the system it installs and controls. In the human spirit of liberty, the algorithm is the enemy."

"So how do you defeat the algorithm?" Lane asked.

"Good question," Rob replied. Although Rob looked like he had an answer, he instead turned to Billy, asking, "Any ideas?"

"Well, I was thinking of having another beer, if that's what you mean," Billy replied with a smile.

Rob and Lane laughed. To the others' surprise, though, Rob added the reply, "Exactly."

"More beer?!" Billy rejoiced, adding, "I'm in. Can we start now?"

Rob and Lane laughed again. But Rob explained, "Not just more beer but anything that transcends the algorithm in a way that encourages others to ignore it."

Billy continued to play along, replying, "So we could have a full-on party!"

Rob nodded with another smile. Lane, though, frowned, saying, "Partying isn't going to stop the algorithm. It's not going to stop the council."

Rob nodded again, replying, "Right. But bold celebrations outside the algorithm will embolden it to overreach its hidden powers, drawing it into the light. And once it's in the light, other powers can decide how to control or crush it."

Lane thought over Rob's last reply while Billy popped open another can of beer. Finally, Lane asked, "What's my role? How can I hasten the algorithm's exposure?"

"Seems like you're already doing so," Rob replied. He paused, wondering whether to say what he was thinking. After a moment's thought, he added, "Let's keep an eye out for Doyle's retaliation. It's coming."

4

Elena was glad she had come to Las Vegas with Marla. She was also glad they'd brought Dani along.

Elena had grown up without a circle of skilled and ambitious women friends. The things that Marla and Dani did surprised and impressed Elena. The things that Marla and Dani thought and said also surprised and impressed Elena. She was gaining confidence in her own insights and ambitions.

Elena had been to a couple of dozen races with Lane already, over the course of the prior year. Attending the race at Las Vegas wasn't anything particularly new. But after the season's break and her own growing introspection, Elena was seeing things anew.

One of the things Elena was seeing at the races was how other women her age were managing both their bold personal and professional ambitions, while also raising families.

Elena's father Raoul had so dominated her mother that her mother had no apparent role other than to care for Elena as she grew up. As soon as Elena was old enough to travel internationally with Raoul, they had just left Elena's mother behind.

Elena hadn't seen professional women with their families in her travels with Raoul. She had met a few business women here and there, and a few female government officials. But their children, if they had any, had generally been nowhere in sight. Most of the women Elena had seen were childless adornments to men, much as she knew she was Raoul's adornment.

If Elena had taken notice the prior year, she would immediately have seen that the stock-car community differed. Working women with children traveled with their husbands. Working women with children also stayed home, managing their family's important affairs.

But until Raoul's arrest and her resettlement with Rob and Marla, Elena hadn't been in any mental or emotional condition to notice the circumstances of the vital stock-car women around her. After the racing season's break, Elena took notice.

The notice Elena took of the vital women around her, often with children, stirred in something Elena hadn't expected. It first stirred an ambition to develop her own skills and capacities to engage with and help others. But it simultaneously stirred a dream that she might also have children for whom to care and to raise in this singular motorsports community.

From the moment she met Lane, Elena had known how successfully Blake and Diana had raised Lane in motorsports. Elena saw in Lane what a woman generally wants to see in a potential husband and father of her children, which is the desire to live joyously, ambitiously, lovingly, and responsibly in a vital community. Blake, Diana, and the motorsports community had fostered Lane's fullest development.

But as Elena got to know Lane's sister Dani, Elena saw that the motorsports community had fully developed Dani, too. Dani shared Lane's confidence, ambition, intelligence, curiosity, and care for others. And in her emerging relationship with Darnell, Dani was also seeing possibilities for her further growth within the same community.

Dani's connection with Lane's teammate Darnell had been a revelation for Elena. When Elena first began dating and then living with Lane, Dani had been leading her own life away from motorsports, learning her skills in the tech field. Elena had barely known her.

When Dani began dating Darnell, Elena felt like she was reliving her own entry into the motorsports community. Elena was watching closely how Dani navigated the complex circumstances of her new relationship.

Yet Elena was doing more than watching. Elena was also speaking with Dani, both learning from Dani while also helping Dani along.

Elena and Dani decided to watch the Las Vegas race from one of the skyboxes Lane's team had secured for sponsors and friends of the team. During the long leadup to the race, they chatted about their personal relationships, as younger women sometimes do.

"What drew you to Darnell?" Elena asked Dani.

Dani looked out across the race track infused with the bright desert sun.

"Kind of scary," Dani admitted, "But he reminds me of my dad."

Elena raised her eyebrows. They both laughed lightly.

"Nothing too wrong with that," Elena replied.

"No," Dani agreed, "I suppose not. I mean, dad is great. It's just, I'd never want Darnell to try to be like my dad."

Elena nodded. She thought for a moment how unlike, and how like, Lane was to her own father Raoul.

Dani and Elena watched as the driver introductions began far below on the track. Dani soon addressed the subject again.

"I never thought I'd date a race driver," she said firmly.

Elena raised her eyebrows again. She tipped her head in curiosity, to encourage Dani to explain. Dani soon did.

"It can be such a *public* thing, you know?" Dani asked.

Elena nodded. She had never feared the public aspect of dating a race driver. Her odd lifestyle traveling all over the world with Raoul had inoculated her against that fear. But Elena certainly understood it. Intimate relationships are supposed to be intimate, not public. Publicity generally does them no good.

Elena thought of something. With a smile on her face to ensure that Dani knew she was joking, Elena asked, "Are you going to be in the victory lane photographs next to Darnell if he wins today?"

"No way!" Dani replied, adding, "Wild horses couldn't drag me there."

"It needs to be a process, doesn't it?" Elena asked kindly.

Dani looked down at her hands on her lap, as they sat watching the driver introductions. Coincidentally, the announcer was just introducing Darnell. Dani and Elena pointed, laughing together.

"He's handsome," Elena said to Dani.

Dani shrugged, saying, "I suppose. I mean, of course, that's nice. But there's a lot of handsome guys around who I wouldn't touch with a ten-foot pole."

They both laughed, nodding. Dani, though, had a question. Turning serious, she asked Elena, "Will you help me through that process? I mean, if Darnell and I continue to date?"

Elena smiled and nodded. Then she reached over and gave Dani a hug. As Elena did so, a strange satisfaction flooded her. She hadn't imagined that anyone, no less Dani, would look to her for advice and support.

Down on the track, driver introductions had ended. The prayer and anthem quickly followed, finally reaching the moment to which Lane looked forward every week, when he could turn his full attention to the race.

Lane climbed into his car. But as he did so, he stopped momentarily. Sitting atop the door's window frame, with his legs inside the car ready to slip in through the window and into his seat, Lane looked up and down pit road at the other drivers. Many of those drivers were kissing their wife, hugging their girlfriend, or handing their little child over to their wife.

Almost involuntarily, Lane thought of Elena. And Lane smiled as he did so. Then, he took a deep breath and slipped into his race car.

Donning his helmet, Lane began to listen to the race radio. Billy confirmed his channel. So did Lane's crew chief. The crew chief asked if Lane was all set. The race director made his radio check. And Lane waited for the grand marshal's command to start the engine.

Lane usually would have been rehearsing his race strategy at that moment. But instead, Doyle and the council popped into his head. Lane looked at the car's gauges, thinking of the data streams they would produce. And he began to think of how the council might alter that data.

For a moment, Lane realized how immersed his driving had become in data. For a moment, he remembered the thrill he'd had when a youth racer, of just feeling the dirt track under the tires of his junior sprint car. Lane remembered the satisfaction of just driving, just challenging one's own sense, not an algorithm's sense, of the capacity of the race car.

The grand marshal's call to start the engine broke Lane's reverie. But a shadow of that reverie remained. Lane had a new race strategy. He would minimize the data influences while maximizing his own feel for the track and car. He would race like he did when a youth.

The early part of the race unfolded without incident. The cars all seemed to be cooperating. No engines blew. No tires failed. And the cars all handled well enough to keep them out of the infield, off the wall, and from sliding into one another.

The drivers began the race cooperating, too, at least to a greater degree than they soon would, when the first stage ended and points battles heated up.

Lane gained a few spots without pushing the issue. He lost fewer spots without having to aggressively defend and block.

Darnell reached Lane's bumper once. Billy had given Lane the car's number. Lane had smiled inside the car when he heard Billy's voice give Darnell's car number. Billy had smiled, too, atop the spotter stand. Lane could hear a hint of Billy's smile in his voice.

Lane prepared to give way to his teammate if Darnell had the clearly faster race car. But after a lap with Darnell at Lane's bumper, another car engaged Darnell from behind, causing Darnell to fall back. Lane did not see Darnell in close quarters again during the race.

As Lane drove, he realized how often his attention was turning away from the track and toward data issues. When Lane started the race, the gauges seemed to galvanize his attention, demanding that he continuously read and process their constant reports. Slowly, though, Lane coaxed himself to pay more attention to the car, track, and competition, letting the gauges do their own work.

Lane also began to distinguish the data his crew chief and Billy were sharing with Lane over the race radio, from their own observations. The crew chief seemed especially captivated by data. The crew chief was sharing not only track temperatures, weather reports, and telemetry data from Lane's car, but telemetry data from other cars, too.

Each Cup race car continuously transmits telemetry data over UHF radio waves to a mobile data center in a semi-truck trailer the stock-car association hauls to each race track. The data provider processes and then retransmits the telemetry data on every Cup race car to each race team. The data provider also shares some telemetry data with race broadcasters and with race fans.

As Lane listened to the radio chatter, he realized that data influenced the crew chief and race engineer more than data influenced him. While he could minimize the data's influence, the data's influence on his race outcome would remain unless the crew chief and race engineer somehow did so, too.

A crash brought out the yellow caution flag and then the red flag for a race stop, while track crew cleaned up debris and fluids that had spread across the track.

Lane sat captive in his car, parked on the track among the other race cars. In the race's lull, Lane began to think of what he might say to his crew chief about moderating the data's influence and how his crew chief would respond.

Lane was certain his crew chief would respond negatively. After all, every member of every race team seemed to believe that the way forward was *more* data, not *less* data. Teams in every sport, stock-car racing certainly included, were hiring more data analysts and giving those analysts more influence, responsibility, and power.

Yet Lane felt the need to recognize and rescue something from that rush to digitize and virtualize the motorsport. Maybe it was only his own pride in his driving skill, his own exalted misunderstanding of his limited role in the whole enterprise. Maybe data did control, and he was only a tiny cog in its great wheel.

But if so, then Lane didn't want to be a part of it. Lane wanted the motorsport to represent something essentially human, not something essentially inhumane. Lane wanted the motorsport to reflect adventure, daring, courage, and the stories of heroes. He didn't want the motorsport to represent a corporate grayness, with its heroic figures drowned in a sea of soulless numbers.

The race radio interrupted Lane's reflection. The drivers restarted their cars and resumed their positions behind the pace car, slowly circling the track. Lane fell dutifully into line. Pit road opened, and the field, Lane included, came down for tires and fuel. And then, the race was back on, lap after lap.

As the laps wore on, Lane regained his confidence in driving. He thought less and felt more. His mind cleared so that his senses could perceive and act. Lane began to get into the flow again of just driving. And he gradually moved forward in the big race pack.

Lane wisely avoided the brief skirmishes at the end of the first stage. He was still too far back to even consider racing for the top-ten stage finish necessary to pick up stage points. But the field's quickening pace and energy at the first stage's end excited Lane, reminding him again of why he raced.

The second stage brought Lane more success. Indeed, Lane briefly felt deserving of his ride.

For the first time with his new team, Lane climbed into the top ten. Race commentators noted that Lane had gained more positions than any other driver in the race. Elena and Dani began to root Lane on from their vantage point in the skybox. Lane's sponsor representatives in the same skybox were all smiles, as the broadcast displayed the corporate logos festooned across Lane's car.

Every race driver knows, though, that gaining positions from the rear or middle of the pack nearer to the front is one thing, while gaining positions within the top five or top ten is a completely different challenge. The cars get faster and better in their handling as one moves forward through the pack. Progress naturally slows or stalls for all but the fastest cars.

Lane rode for the rest of stage two at the back end of the top ten. He even gained his first stage point, fending off another driver's late challenge to finish tenth at the end of stage two. For a second-year driver with a new team, that first stage point was a significant step.

A natural next significant step would be to finish in the top ten or fifteen, on the same lap as the leaders. Finishing races is the mark of a competent team. Finishing in the top ten or fifteen is the mark of a strong team.

Elena and Dani cheered Lane on as the third and final stage began.

For the restart, though, Lane and the other drivers earning stage points had fallen back ten spots to lead-lap cars that had pitted just before stage two's end. That meant Lane started the final stage back in the middle of the pack, without any great tire advantage.

Elena and Dani didn't know it, but Lane wasn't on a particularly good strategy for a strong finish. The nine cars immediately ahead of Lane were the nine cars that had beaten Lane at the end of stage two. They were all faster cars with better handling. To gain any positions,

Lane would have to pass those faster cars. And ten more lead-lap cars were ahead of them.

Lane thus ran lap after lap in the middle of the pack. Lane wasn't frustrated in doing so. He understood the race strategy. His crew chief could have brought him in for tires and fuel before the stage's end. Doing so could have put Lane in the lead or near the lead for the final stage's restart.

But doing so would also have sacrificed the top-ten stage finish and its stage point. The crew chief had judged the top-ten stage finish and point worth more than restarting up front, with nine faster cars further behind. Lane, in other words, took the spoils early, sacrificing a restart lead that Lane likely soon would have relinquished to faster cars behind.

Lane thus just wanted to finish the race, not even expecting to do so back in the top ten. Unfortunately, a race finish was not to be Lane's case.

Lane steered well clear of the other cars battling for position around him. He wanted to avoid a wreck, even if it meant giving up a handful of positions. Yet halfway through the final stage, Lane's temperature gauge showed an alarming rise, indicating an overheating engine and the risk of a blown engine.

Lane and his crew chief conferred over the race radio. Billy saw nothing on the grill of Lane's car. Race video showed the grill to be clear of clogging debris. And the engine appeared to be running fine. Lane detected no falloff in engine performance. But the temperature gauge showed the engine temperature continuing to rise until it reached the level for the engine to fail.

"Back it down," the crew chief radioed Lane.

Lane hesitated. He wanted to ignore the data. But he didn't want to blow the engine and, in doing so, imperil his relationship with the crew chief and his new team. So Lane eased up on the accelerator. Cars began to pass Lane's car, one by one. Lane fell well back.

The temperature gauge, though, didn't show any change in temperature. Indeed, the gauge showed a continuing rise.

"Bring it in," the crew chief radioed Lane.

Lane dutifully maneuvered the car onto pit road, as the rest of the field flew by. In the pit stall, the pit crew quickly checked the car's grill, opened the hood, and checked the fan and ducts. Nothing seemed awry.

"Take it back to the garage," the crew chief radioed Lane.

Lane shook his head but followed the crew chief's instructions, pulling the car down pit lane and through the gateway to drive back to the race garage.

As Lane pulled the car into the race garage, he saw a tall figure standing outside the garage. The figure wore a broad smile.

As Lane wrestled his way out of his helmet, gloves, HANS device, and other race gear inside his car, Lane couldn't quite place the smiling figure. Then he remembered. It was Doyle. Lane also remembered Doyle's threat.

Lane's blood began to rise as he climbed hurriedly from his car, ready to challenge Doyle. But when Lane finally climbed out and turned to the garage doorway where Doyle had stood, he was gone.

5

"Nothing wrong with it," the crew chief answered Lane's query about his car's temperature gauge.

Lane shook his head, asking again, "It was a perfectly good gauge?"

"That's what the manufacturer confirmed this morning," the crew chief replied, adding, "We could just as well put it back in the car."

"You're not serious," Lane replied incredulously.

"No, I'm not serious," the crew chief agreed, adding, "But the gauge was perfectly fine."

It was already Tuesday afternoon, two days after the Las Vegas race. The drivers and key personnel had made it home to Charlotte from Las Vegas, ready to test and strategize for the next race at Phoenix Raceway, using more simulator data.

The haulers, their race cars, and their equipment had headed straight for Phoenix Speedway, along with other crew members, rather than make the long drive home to Charlotte, only to have to immediately turn around for Phoenix.

Lane's team, though, had shipped the offending temperature gauge directly to the manufacturer for testing late Monday and early Tuesday. The team had detected no engine issue or other reason for the gauge showing a catastrophic temperature. It must have been the gauge, except that it wasn't.

"What are you going to do about it?" Lane asked after a long pause. He didn't know what else to say, without disclosing his belief that Doyle and his council had altered the gauge's data.

"No idea, frankly," the crew chief said, adding, "Let me get back to you on that one."

Lane nodded. He had a few ideas of his own, ones though that he wasn't quite ready to disclose to his crew chief or race team. He first needed to speak with Rob, Elena, and Dani.

Lane and Dani joined Elena at Rob and Marla's house that evening, according to their new Tuesday evening custom. With the weather still chilly, they gathered around the kitchen table, catching up on personal news and views.

Dani shared with the group a little impression of her time in Las Vegas with Darnell. Dani was just beginning to get comfortable discussing Darnell with her family members, although that process would need more time. As Dani did so, Elena, sitting next to Lane, put her hand on Lane's arm. They looked at one another with smiles.

Darnell had finished the race well back in the pack, without any signs of success and with several reasons for disappointment and even frustration. Dani shared, though, that Darnell had taken the loss and challenges with perfect poise or, more like the fun-loving Darnell, with perfect good humor.

Listening to Dani describe Darnell's equanimity, Lane admitted to himself that he hadn't taken his own

Las Vegas race's outcome, in which he had failed to finish the race due, of all things, to the malfunction of his car's temperature gauge, with equal poise. Lane's result had angered him, anger he had barely concealed.

But as Rob, Marla, Dani, and Elena were about to find out, Lane's anger wasn't over the result itself, nor even over the temperature gauge's malfunction. Lane's anger was over Doyle's threat and the delight that Doyle appeared to have taken in carrying it out through a manipulation of the temperature gauge.

Rob was the first to broach the issue.

"So Darnell lost but didn't succumb," Rob summarized Dani's disclosure for her with an appreciative smile. Rob then turned to Lane, adding, "How about you, Rough Rider?"

Lane smiled at Rob's name for him, something he hadn't heard Rob use before.

"That's about how I feel," Lane replied good naturedly despite his inner anger, explaining, "Assuming that rough riders are those who break wild horses for a living."

Everyone around the table laughed. Glad for the moment's levity, Lane then resumed.

"You know, Doyle was back at the race garage with a big smile when I left the race track," he shared.

Everyone raised their eyebrows. Rob asked, "What do you make of that?"

"I didn't get to ask him," Lane disclosed, adding, "He disappeared before I could get out of the car."

"So what do you infer?" Rob asked again.

"It doesn't leave me much choice but to think that he had something to do with the gauge's failure," Lane answered.

"Or that he wanted you to think so," Elena interjected.

Rob and Marla, both special-operations veterans, having met through their joint service, looked at one another with a knowing nod. Elena was exactly right. Those who seek control over others use such ploys to gain the response they want.

Lane looked at Elena, not with confusion or in disagreement but with respect. Earlier in their relationship, Lane would have resisted Elena's insights. He had since learned to value and even trust her insights.

Lane turned to Rob, asking, "Is that what you think?"

"Could be," Rob answered. He elaborated, "Doyle and the council might have that ability, and Doyle may have exercised it to produce a response in you. Or he and the council may have no such ability or simply not have used that ability against you. But Doyle evidently still wants you to think so."

Lane nodded in agreement. He understood the implication of Rob's point: how Lane responded was more important than what Doyle did or could do. Lane must not relinquish control to Doyle, no matter what Doyle could do. But Lane had another question for Rob.

"So, what do I do?" Lane asked.

Rob paused to frame his response. He looked at Marla, who took his glance as encouragement to jump in.

"Your actions will depend on the circumstances," Marla began. She added, "You must not relinquish control to the council. To avoid giving in to Doyle's manipulation, you must befriend what you don't know rather than trust what you believe you know."

Lane looked at Marla with an air of incredulity. Mouth slightly agape and shaking his head, he said simply, "Oh boy, here we go."

Everyone laughed. Lane had indeed in part meant his comment to be humorous. But he also felt his grasp, which wasn't all that solid in the first place, slipping quickly further away. Marla, though, threw Lane a life line.

"In these mysterious or deceptive situations, recognizing what you don't know is your greater hope than jumping to conclusions and trusting in what you believe you know," Marla explained. She added, "Keep looking at what you don't know, from which you will draw your best options."

Lane began to see a light at the end of his tunnel. Rob chimed in.

"Problems arise because we don't know, not because we know," Rob concurred. He continued, "So befriend what you don't know."

Lane smiled, joking, "Howdy, friend. Nice not to meet you."

Again, everyone laughed. But Rob wasn't done.

"The challenge Doyle and the council have presented you is to perceive reality," Rob resumed. He continued, "Reality involves three fundamental interacting structures. The first structure is potential or, if you prefer, chaos or entropy."

"I sure know chaos," Lane interjected. The others smiled.

"The second structure is the conscious active agent," Rob resumed, adding, "In this instance, that's you."

"That's me, alright," Lane replied, drawing chuckles from the others again.

"And the third structure is the hierarchical order you impose," Rob concluded. To put it all together, he summarized, "In your active consciousness, you draw your preferred order out of the chaos, or range of potential outcomes each with their own probabilities, that you encounter. It's the story of the conquering hero."

"Sounds even more like me," Lane replied, continuing to play along to the smiles and chuckles of the others.

Dani, though, had a question, asking Rob, "I thought reality was something material like this table." Dani knocked on the table with her knuckles, then added, "And the reality here would be whether or not Doyle made Lane drop out of the race."

"No," Rob replied, explaining, "That's too limited a view of reality. The materialist's space-time construct of reality is too limiting of a concept, ignoring more fundamental things that time and space do not explain or control."

Rob's comment drew blank stares all the way around the table. He tried again, saying, "Reality isn't a space-time construct but instead a function of grasping conditions."

Again, Rob saw nothing but blank stares around the table. So he tried once again, saying, "You've heard the expression *to get a grip*?"

Everyone nodded.

"Well then," Rob resumed, "That's what I mean. See, Lane must both grip the steering wheel and get a grip on the data streams he must interpret to succeed in racing, right?"

Again, everyone nodded.

"Well," Rob continued, "Neither the steering wheel nor the data stream are reality. They are both just constructs in the gripping system Lane must employ to draw the highest potential order out of the greatest entropy or chaos he can encounter. Remember, reality isn't material things or conceptual constructs. Reality is Lane's conscious agency drawing preferred order out of the potential he encounters."

Lane smiled at Rob's revelation but still looked like he wasn't sure. So Lane replied, "If that's so, then give me something practical to do with this deeper reality."

"Sure," Rob replied, "That's the easier part. In fact, you've already begun."

Lane gave Rob a confused look, asking, "What have I already done?"

"You've recognized and challenged one of the mediating systems," Rob replied, adding, "You've seen that data flows aren't necessarily reliable. And you've begun to trust again your unmediated intuition, which by the way is the highest form of knowledge."

Lane smiled broadly. Rob was right. That's exactly what Lane had been wanting to do and trying to do.

Rob, though, gave it one last try, saying, "We encounter the infinite creator when looking deeply enough and low enough into his creation, trusting his mediation for the discernment we need to discern, enjoy, share, and celebrate his highest order."

Lane pushed his chair back from the table with an even broader smile. He looked at Elena. She was smiling, too. They laughed with one another. Dani looked from Lane to Elena, smiling warmly at them both.

"Oh, and by the way," Rob added, "I'm continuing to work on the data-security question."

Lane nodded.

"Dessert, anyone?" Marla asked.

The drivers, crew chief, and others who had returned to Charlotte for the short week were soon off again, this time to rejoin their teams and haulers at Phoenix Raceway. Marla, Elena, and Dani stayed home this time. Lane and Darnell would race without their girlfriends Elena and Dani present to support them.

Practice went well enough for Lane. He and his crew chief felt that they had gotten both a literal and figurative grip on the handling Lane preferred for the car. As Lane ran practice lap after practice lap, the car seemed to have taken well to the challenging configuration of the Phoenix track's odd layout.

At one mile around, Phoenix is a *tweener* track, half between the traditional mile-and-a-half tracks that dominate the schedule and the short tracks as short as just a half mile. Phoenix Raceway is neither a high-speed oval nor a bump-and-grind short track. It is a low-banked, mid-speed, tri-oval layout that challenges both cars and drivers.

Phoenix Raceway challenges the cars in their grip and handling around the low-banked, wide-sweeping curves, in their nearly constant acceleration and braking, and in the way that the cars can bottom out when their drivers take the shortcut across the wide skirt of the tri-oval. Phoenix Raceway beats up and wears out equipment.

Phoenix Raceway also beats up and wears out drivers. The track barely allows drivers any place to momentarily relax, perhaps only up the short straightaway, except there, drivers must pass if they can, while jockeying for critical position to enter the tricky grandstand curve. And the layout has one especially difficult turn coming out of the tri-oval, where the wall seems to leap out at cars to slam them, if the driver hasn't perfectly gauged the turn or another car has nudged the victim ever so slightly outward.

Lane stayed off the wall and out of trouble in practice. He was ready for qualifying.

Lane would need to qualify well. Phoenix is also a track where passing can be difficult and blocking easier. Other than the tri-oval shortcut, the track may not offer a lot of options for racing lines, especially before the higher line around the outside of the turns comes in later in the race. Qualifying and track position are thus premium advantages.

Lane slipped away from the track alone for a fast-food break, to think about his qualifying approach. A familiar voice greeted Lane, as he carried his food to a table.

"Want to join me?" Fred asked.

Lane was glad to see Fred, a stock-car association official but also a longtime family friend and licensed psychologist, among other good things. Outside of his official duties, Fred served as a confidante and informal counselor to many within the racing community. He had helped Lane and Elena through their own challenges the prior year.

"How's it going?" Fred asked Lane as Lane took a seat across from him in the booth.

"It's going," Lane replied with a wan smile.

"Not an easy thing, joining a new race team," Fred suggested, adding, "Especially taking a famous father's seat."

Lane repeated the same wan smile. He added, "And I wish it were only that."

"It's never *only that*, is it?" Fred agreed, offering, "Anything else you want to share?"

Lane paused before saying, "Not really, at least not yet. Rob's working on some things."

"I know," Fred replied, to Lane's surprise. Seeing Lane's surprise, Fred smiled, saying, "Oh, you don't think Rob would have shared that with me or that I would have heard it somewhere else?"

Lane looked up from his food at Fred with an apologetic smile, saying, "Of course you would have heard of it."

"Hard fighting a hidden enemy, isn't it?" Fred asked. When Lane nodded, Fred offered, "Want some advice?"

Lane nodded again.

"Accept the full weight of the things that befall you, even unfair things," Fred began.

Lane nodded but replied, "Not much else one can do, right?"

"Oh," Fred replied, "People do lots of other things, like cry and complain and rebel and quit, although I'd not expect you to do any of those things."

Lane nodded. They each took another bite of their fast food. Fred then continued.

"Embracing the full weight of unfair things carries the potential not just for enduring but for growing through those things."

Lane interrupted, asking, "What if those things are the fault or even the evil of others?"

"Doesn't change things much," Fred replied. Lane raised his eyebrows in surprise, so Fred explained, "No matter the cause of the challenge, embracing it activates your growth, literally alerting your DNA to help you develop new capacities."

Lane again raised his eyebrows but this time with a nod of appreciation. He liked the idea of developing new capacities. He knew he needed to do so.

Fred took another bite of fast food before musing, "You know, it can be even better if the challenge you overcome is the consequence of another's evil."

"How so?" Lane asked with a note of disbelief.

"Confronting a vicious entity allows you to triumph over that same evil within you," Fred replied, adding, "Think of it as if you only conquer within yourself those things that confront you. If another's fault confronts you, then you have the opportunity to overcome the same fault within you. If another's evil confronts you, then you have the opportunity to overcome that same evil within you."

Lane huffed, saying, "If that's so, then one would want the greater, not the lesser challenges."

"Exactly so," Fred said to Lane's surprise. Fred continued, "It's the story of the hero's adventure. The smaller the adventure, the less the hero achieves, and the less the hero grows."

They both fell silent, thinking of what Fred had said. After a minute, Fred continued.

"The higher the goal, the greater the joy in progress toward it. We experience joy not by attaining goals but by positing them, pursuing them, and seeing progress toward them. Ideals generate goals, which generate joy."

"I'm not feeling all that joyous," Lane replied wryly.

"That's because you haven't seen progress yet toward your goal," Fred replied, adding, "But you will, soon."

"Promise?" Lane asked, laughing.

"I can't promise it," Fred replied, "But I can sure see it, and I think you do, too."

Lane nodded. He did expect progress, both with his new race team and with the data issues. Lane just didn't know how soon.

Just then, a veteran Cup driver walked by their booth.

"Hey," Lane rose quickly to greet the driver with a big smile and an offered handshake. Lane added, "Let me know sometime if you'd like me to come on your podcast."

The veteran driver shook Lane's hand warmly but replied, "Not happening. I don't have a podcast anymore."

"What do you mean?" Lane asked incredulously. The podcast had been among the most popular among race fans.

"That new data provider shut it down," the veteran driver said, adding, "Apparently, we weren't satisfying their algorithm."

Lane bristled, shaking his head in anger. The veteran driver gave a brief waved and walked off with his fast food.

Lane sat back down across from Fred who said bemusedly, "Looks like your challenge is spreading to other drivers."

6

Lane's strategy for the Phoenix Raceway Cup race, the fourth of the new season, was paying off.

Lane had qualified his best of the season, well into the front half of the pack. Lane had once again qualified ahead of Darnell. Lane had also qualified ahead of one of his two veteran teammates. Lane was confident that his crew chief and engineer were getting a sense of how to set up the car for him, even for the difficult Phoenix Raceway layout.

Lane had settled again on a strategy of minimizing the influence of data while maximizing his intuitive racing skills. Lane had two reasons for taking that approach. The first reason was that he no longer trusted the data. If Doyle and his council were indeed influencing race outcomes, they weren't influencing them in Lane's favor. Their warnings and Doyle's glee at Lane's Las Vegas loss seemed clearly enough to indicate so.

But whether Doyle and his council were manipulating the race data or not, Lane was also thinking of Rob's insight that intuitive knowledge, more so than derived knowledge, was its highest form. Lane wanted to trust the transcendent, the through line that preceded distortion and overcame deception. Lane wanted to receive knowledge from the consciousness beyond creation. He wanted to race transcendently, above whatever challenges the race's entropy presented.

And that was how the race had so far proceeded. Driving with a clarity, courage, and confidence that he had barely felt before, Lane had gradually gained track positions throughout the first two stages of the race, even though passing was so difficult on the odd Phoenix layout.

In the later stages of the race, once he had gained the top ten, Lane was glad that passing was difficult. All he had to do was hold his position, which his well-handling car seemed fully capable of doing, while looking for whatever clear opportunities the race presented for him to gain even more positions.

The leaders came down pit road for their last green-flag pit stops. Lane followed them in, on the bumper of the car immediately in front of him. Four tires, fuel, and Lane followed the same car right back out onto the track. Lane's car once again leapt to life, as Lane prepared to reel in more cars ahead of him.

But then, the radio call came. Lane had sped entering pit road. Lane would have to serve a pass-through penalty, returning down pit road under the green flag. Lane would lose at least a dozen positions, falling so far back as to effectively end his race.

"That's impossible," Lane radioed back to his crew chief as he continued to circle the track.

"They've now confirmed it," the crew chief soon radioed back, adding, "Bring it in this time, if you can."

"But I was in line behind the cars ahead of me the whole time," Lane complained, "I couldn't have sped unless they all did, too. Are they calling them in?"

"That's a negative," the crew chief replied wryly as Lane missed pit road again and continued on around the track. The crew chief added, "You've got to bring it in next time around or they'll black flag you."

Lane drew to the inside of the track and slowed down the backstretch to draw tight around the bottom of the turn for pit road entry. Down pit road Lane came. By the time he was back up to speed on the track, he was nearer the back of the pack than the front of the pack. Although he fought valiantly on, his race was over. He finished in twenty-fifth place.

Lane pulled his car back to the garage for the team to load it on the hauler. It would be a long trip back to Charlotte. Lane headed to the motorhome to shower and change for his flight back.

As Lane approached the motorhome, he saw a familiar figure emerge from the back seat of a sleek, white, electric-powered sedan with dark tinted windows, parked alongside the motorhome. It was Doyle.

"Good race," Doyle greeted Lane, adding with a sly smile, "Too bad about the speeding penalty."

Lane stopped in his tracks, bristling, with fists clenched. He wanted to emit a flood of accusations. And he wanted to punch Doyle's leering face.

But something deep inside Lane whispered to be still. Lane briefly thought of the advice he'd had from both Rob and Fred. And he thought of Marla's warning not to relinquish control to Doyle. Embrace the unknown rather than assume one knows. So Lane just stood, glaring at Doyle, trying to ignore his rising blood pressure and roiling emotions.

"Anything I can do for you?" Doyle offered.

"Leave me alone," Lane replied through gritted teeth, adding, "You know I wasn't speeding. I just want a fair chance to win."

"Oh, we can certainly arrange that," Doyle replied with another sly smile, adding, "We just need your cooperation."

Lane looked at Doyle in shock. Doyle was offering to fix a race.

Doyle, though, stared far off over Lane's head, as if Lane was but an insignificant foreground anomaly. As Doyle did so, he used his peripheral vision to study Lane's reaction for the expected response. Lane let a moment's surprise escape his control but then quickly covered it up with anger. Doyle noted both responses, just as he expected.

Lane could feel that he was losing control. He even sensed that Doyle wanted him to do so. So rather than say or do something he'd later regret, Lane turned away from Doyle, flung open the motorhome door, and climbed the stairs inside.

As Lane did so, he heard Doyle call after him in a mockingly sing-song voice, "Let me know if you change your mind!"

Lane glanced out the motorhome's window as he headed to the back for his shower and change. One of the council's android-like figures had emerged from the driver's seat of the sleek white vehicle to open the rear door for Doyle. But Doyle paused to glance up at the motorhome's heavily tinted window with a big smile, before climbing in the vehicle.

Lane shook his head. He could hardly believe Doyle's hubris.

Lane showered and changed quickly. Rob was already waiting outside the motorhome with a ride to the airport, where Lane would catch the team owner's private jet back to Charlotte with the team's other three drivers.

"Impressions?" Rob asked after Lane had settled in next to Rob in the vehicle's front passenger seat.

"You mean of the race?" Lane asked.

Rob nodded. Lane breathed a deep sigh before answering.

"I guess I'm encouraged about the racing," Lane finally replied, adding, "Just not the ridiculous penalty or the race result."

Lane looked at Rob. Rob stole a glance back as he wheeled the vehicle out of the grounds and toward the airport.

"I wasn't speeding," Lane said.

"I know you weren't," Rob replied.

"That's proof that something's up with Doyle and the council, isn't it?" Lane asked.

"Not proof," Rob replied, adding, "Just potential evidence. Plenty of drivers have had penalties they didn't really deserve, whether due to official misinterpretations, measurement failures, or a confluence of anomalies."

Lane pressed his lips together in frustration. He then told Rob about his encounter with Doyle including Doyle's suggestion that he could arrange a race win.

"What do you make of that?" Lane asked.

"Well," Rob replied, "It does prove Doyle's desire that you believe he is capable of doing so. It doesn't prove anything else yet."

Rob paused before asking, "How'd you handle it?"

"Walked away," Lane said.

"Good," Rob said. They smiled at one another. Within minutes, they were at the airport and each on their way home to Charlotte.

To Lane's surprise, Elena was at his condominium door early the next morning.

"Thought I'd give you a ride to the race facility," Elena said with a coy smile as Lane opened the door to greet her. They looked at one another with matching smiles.

"I missed you," they both said simultaneously. They laughed and hugged in a long, warm embrace, ending with a rich kiss.

"Dinner out this evening?" Lane invited Elena as they eased out of their embrace.

"You're on," Elena replied, adding, "Except it's going to be a double date."

Lane scrunched his face at Elena in question. Elena just smiled back at Lane. Then Lane realized what was up. He rolled his eyes and shook his head humorously.

"Dani and Darnell," Lane said matter of factly.

Elena nodded, her smile growing. Lane dropped his head, shaking it once again.

"So this is how it's going to be?" Lane asked, again with a clear hint of humor.

Elena laughed, saying only, "Yes. We'll pick you up at the race facility at six."

Lane shrugged. They both laughed. Instead of heading to Elena's car, though, they resumed their warm embrace.

Lane walked into his crew chief's office at the race facility a short while later. Lane was about to sit down when the crew chief interrupted him.

"Boss wants to see you," the crew chief said with a tip of his head in the direction of the team owner's office.

Lane raised his eyebrows and held up both palms, silently asking the crew chief if he knew what might be up. The crew chief shook his head and shrugged.

"Back soon," Lane said, adding with a wry smile, "I hope."

The crew chief chuckled, saying, "I'll be waiting."

Lane made his way to the team owner's office. The team owner's administrative assistant greeted Lane as he entered the suite.

"He's waiting for you," she said with a smile.

Lane took a deep breath. It would be his first official solo post-race meeting with the team owner.

"It'll be alright," the assistant assured Lane with another smile. She rose to open the door for Lane to the owner's inner office.

Lane gave a weak smile back, along with a shrug. Putting his hands in his pockets, and dropping his head, Lane walked into the office.

"Have a seat, Big Boy," the team owner greeted Lane warmly, while motioning to a leather chair in front of the owner's vast desk.

Lane took a seat in the chair, feeling like a school child called to the principal's office.

"Tell me about your race yesterday," the team owner invited Lane.

Lane thought he detected a clear note of encouragement in the owner's invitation. So he tried to focus first on the positives.

"I think we're coming together as a team," Lane began.

The owner smiled and nodded. Lane even thought the owner quietly breathed, "Seems so," although Lane wasn't quite sure because his blood pressure had his ears ringing and his heart pounding. But Lane continued.

"I think we're getting better setups already," Lane said, as his head cleared a little of the nervousness he had felt when first entering the owner's office. Lane added, "And I think I'm driving with more clarity and confidence."

"Tell me about your driving," the owner asked with a small lean forward, indicating his earnest interest.

The team owner had once been a noted race driver, not coming up through the ranks like young drivers today but as a business owner with a passion for racing and the means to fund it. The owner hadn't raced in the stock-car association's top divisions but had raced in other well-regarded series where professional drivers and top amateurs compete, regionally, nationally, and even internationally.

Realizing the owner's interest, Lane opened up. He began by explaining, "I've had the sense that I've been racing with too great of an analytical focus on the data points. I've been thinking more than feeling."

The owner nodded as a smile spread across his face. This time, Lane heard the owner clearly say, "Yes, that's a temptation and problem, isn't it?"

Lane smiled back and nodded. Knowing the owner's racing experience and reputation, Lane didn't want to sound like he knew it all. But he also didn't want to put the owner on the spot. So timidly, he asked, "You know what I mean? I mean, you've experienced that?"

Lane blushed, embarrassed that he had at first made it sound like the owner might not even have understood such a simple point.

"Oh, I know what you mean," the owner said in a kindly manner, ignoring Lane's blush. The owner continued, "I've been exactly there several times, where I had to get back to racing more by the seat of my pants."

They were both silent for a moment. The owner, though, soon continued.

"Here's the way I think your uncle Rob might put it."

The owner paused with a chuckle. Lane nodded and smiled, too. They both knew and appreciated Rob's way of putting things. The owner then resumed.

"Race driving is really a search for a signal transcendence. Driving demands that we notice these rare inklings of ultimate reality."

The owner paused again with another chuckle. He asked Lane, "How am I doing? Sound like your uncle?"

The owner smiled at his own articulation. Lane laughed, nodding vigorously and hoping that the owner would continue. The owner soon did.

"But at most," the owner resumed, "We only perceive signals of transcendence. And that limit is for our own good. To glimpse full transcendence would fracture us in a way we cannot countenance nor control."

The owner's insight spurred a question in Lane, who asked, "What role, then, do we allow for technology, for data, when racing by the seat of our pants?"

"Exactly the question," the owner replied appreciatively. After a moment's pause, he ventured, "The first transcendent image must be uncut, untouched. Technology and its data may only then be transcendence's intermediary."

Tipping his head to consider the owner's premise, Lane replied with satisfaction, "Sounds about right."

The owner and Lane smiled at one another.

"Alright then," the owner summarized, "We've got ourselves some direction in this little snafu over gauges, speeding penalties, and data conspiracies."

Lane raised his eyebrows in surprise. He hadn't said anything about Doyle and the council. But of course, the team owner had his sources. He must have known all along. Lane moved as if to go, not wanting to overstay his welcome.

"One more thing," the owner said. Lane settled back into his seat.

"I know it's early in the season and that we're now an especially young team," the owner began.

Lane silently gulped, sensing what was coming.

The owner continued, "But we're already under some sponsor pressure for better results. That doesn't mean we're changing anything. We've just asked sponsors to hold on until after the Darlington race, halfway through the regular season. We'll have some better results by then."

The owner looked Lane straight in the eyes but with the same kindness he had shown when discussing race driving.

Just to be sure Lane understood, the owner added, "That's in no sense a warning. We trust you, Darnell, and our veteran drivers. We just don't sugar-coat things around here."

Lane nodded. Sensing that the meeting was over, he rose and started to turn for the door. But he stopped, turned back, and said quietly, "Thank you."

The owner looked up at Lane with the same kind smile, saying, "Well no. Thank you."

They both smiled and laughed.

Lane peaked into Darnell's office on his way back to see his crew chief. Darnell had his feet up on his desk, looking at a tablet. Seeing Lane, he put the tablet aside and, giving Lane a weak smile, waved Lane into the office.

"How's it going?" Lane asked. Lane was wondering if Darnell had a similar meeting with the team owner that morning.

"Not so good," Darnell replied, shaking his head.

"What's up?" Lane asked, concerned that Darnell might have drawn something more dire from a meeting with the team owner that morning.

"I've lost a sponsor," Darnell replied.

Lane raised his eyebrows in alarm. The owner hadn't said anything about already losing sponsors. The owner had only mentioned sponsor pressure.

"Hard to believe after only four races," Lane mused.

"No," Darnell corrected Lane, "It has nothing to do with our race results."

"Then what?" Lane asked in disbelief.

"Apparently, the tech company running things around here has an algorithm that rejects certain sponsors," Darnell replied.

"What?" Lane asked again in shock, "The council has terminated your sponsor?"

"I don't know about any council," Darnell replied, adding, "The explanation we got sounded something like sponsor misalignment with approved values."

Lane shook his head.

"Look," Darnell added, "We'll be alright. As soon as we pick up the pace around here, another sponsor is sure to step in."

Lane nodded. Looking at Darnell, Lane wanted more than ever to help his teammate succeed. Extending his hand to Darnell, Lane replied, "Let's do that. Let's pick up the pace around here. By Darlington, halfway through the season, at least one of us will have been in victory lane."

Darnell nodded, giving Lane a firm handshake. Wanting to change the subject, Darnell asked, "Dinner tonight?"

"Yes, I've heard," Lane replied. He gave Darnell a big smile, saying, "Double date."

7

"So how was the double date last night?" Marla asked Lane with a twinkle in her eye, as Lane joined Rob, Dani, and Elena around the kitchen table for their customary Tuesday evening time.

"Late," Lane said as he yawned, adding with looks toward Dani and Elena, "Some had more energy than others."

Dani and Elena laughed. Dani chimed in saying, "Our driver boys were a little tired."

Lane shook his head wearily, saying to Dani and Elena, "We may have to put you two on the simulator for a few laps, to wear you out first, before the next time."

"Oh," Marla replied with a mischievous grin toward Dani and Elena, "So there's going to be a next time. Well, that's good news."

Lane rolled his eyes humorously as Dani and Elena laughed again. But then Lane had a thought, suggesting, "Maybe Darnell should just join us here next week."

Lane looked at Marla who looked at Rob. Rob shrugged, after which Marla said, "I guess let's give it a try."

Dani brightened. Elena smiled, placing a kind hand on Dani's shoulder.

Rob soon brought assorted entrees in from the grill on the patio outside. As everyone ate, Marla shared stories of how her race team with Lane's dad Blake was faring in the level below Lane's top Cup series. Lane was glad for the diversion, although it wouldn't last long.

"If you all don't mind," Rob interjected when everyone had finished eating and conversation had subsided, "Lane and I have a little business to discuss."

Lane raised his eyebrows. He hadn't heard yet what Rob had in mind.

"You gentlemen are excused," Marla said, adding humorously, "We ladies have our own business to discuss."

Elena and Dani laughed appreciatively.

Rob and Lane headed to the den where, as they settled in, Rob apologized, "Sorry to turn pleasure to business, but I didn't know when I'd catch you otherwise."

Lane nodded, saying, "No problem. I'm all ears."

"We're ready for the next step in our investigation of this data manipulation issue," Rob began.

"Well good," Lane replied, adding with a note of irritation, "I've been feeling more than a little *left out alone* dealing with that issue."

"That's been intentional," Rob said, "Although my saying so is probably little comfort to you."

Lane chuckled, shaking his head and saying, "No, that doesn't make me feel any better."

Lane huffed after another moment's thought, adding, "Makes me feel a little worse, in fact."

Rob nodded, explaining, "Catching a deceiver unfortunately requires deception. You're not out there alone. We've been working on things. But we've wanted Doyle and the council to think you're out there alone."

"I get it," Lane nodded, adding with another chuckle, "But it still doesn't make me feel any better."

Both were silent for a moment until Lane asked, "Okay, so what's the plan?"

Lane listened carefully, asking questions here and there, as Rob explained what he had in mind.

When Rob was done, he asked, "So, are you in?"

"Do I have any choice?" Lane asked with a wry smile. He then added, "Of course I'm in. Let's just hope it works."

Rob paused, looking at Lane to be sure he had Lane's full attention. Rob then replied, "It's not going to work like you think. It will just be the first of several deeply disruptive iterations. This one's going to be harder than the last one."

Lane raised his eyebrows with a look of surprise and concern. He said, "You mean harder than Raoul's arrest?"

"Yes," Rob replied with dead seriousness.

"Why?" Lane asked, correcting himself and adding, "I mean, how?"

"First, more is at stake," Rob explained. He continued, "Second, the opposition has far greater resources and sophistication. The politics of it are also much more difficult. And the opposition's commitment is deeper, more profound."

Lane gave Rob a curious look. After a moment, Lane replied, "I can see everything but your last point."

Rob gathered his thoughts to explain. He began, "Raoul was money laundering. He had no pretense of commitment to it other than the means it generated and lifestyle it sustained."

Lane nodded. He could almost imagine Raoul as just another victim of the corruption his money laundering supported, not as a perpetrator, surely not an architect, of that corruption. Raoul was the non-innocent bystander, the one who decided to profit from the wrongs he observed from a distance. Raoul was culpable, but culpability has degrees. His residence was not at the root of hell, just at its doorstep.

Lane still wasn't sure, though, where Doyle, the council, and their algorithm fit in the assessment of their wrongs. They weren't doing any of the horrible things from which Raoul had indirectly profited, like trafficking and drug dealing. At worst, they were profiting from data manipulation, at Lane's expense and the expense of others.

"So how is Doyle's commitment any deeper than Raoul's?" Lane asked.

Lane noticed Rob take a deep breath before speaking. So Lane interjected with a brief smile, "Oh boy, here it comes."

Rob smiled back before beginning his explanation, "We put our creator at the mountaintop, from material at the base all the way up to his meaning at the top. Our creator is not only a point and principle but also a person, both fully human and divine. You and I trust that our creator moves us up the mountain as long as we keep him at its top."

Rob paused only a moment before continuing, "Raoul, though, had no one at his mountaintop other than himself. He was a guy on the make for himself. An adversary who only pursues his own interests isn't the greatest adversary because his pursuit is ultimately alone. His only allies are also in it for themselves and thus untrustworthy."

Lane nodded. He knew exactly what Rob meant. Raoul had no one to help him other than those who believed they were helping themselves. Rob then continued.

"Doyle, though, puts the algorithm at the mountaintop, as many others do. He has a god, one infinitely less powerful than our own but formidable nonetheless, especially in that many others will follow along."

Rob stopped, letting Lane digest the thought. Lane had a question, though.

"What really is this algorithm, though?" Lane asked, adding, "People don't worship a formula."

"You're right, in a way," Rob replied, explaining, "The algorithm isn't really the thing. Instead, it's their totalizing way of looking at things."

Lane gave Rob a confused look, so Rob explained.

"Our creator's mountain base, where all material resides, is not only incredibly broad but also good. Our good creator made a good creation, although broken in its fall. Our creator's desires order and prioritize things up the mountain, leaving its broad base, margins, and boundaries as vital potential out of which to refresh his order. Our creator loves all creation, drawing his exquisite meaning by ordering disordered material."

Lane nodded as Rob paused, so Rob continued.

"The algorithm is a distorted perspective of that reality. The algorithm purports to supplant the good creator at the mountaintop. The algorithm makes order the god at the mountaintop."

Rob stopped, too soon for Lane's curious mind.

"Why can't they just leave us alone?" Lane prompted Rob, adding, "Why cancel podcasts, reject sponsors, and retaliate against anyone, like me, who seems to challenge them?"

"When order is your tyrannical god at the mountaintop," Rob replied, "You naturally treat the mountain's disordered base not as rich potential out of which to refresh order but as an irritant and enemy to destroy."

"So I've been the irritant," Lane observed quietly.

"Of course," Rob replied, "And you've known so."

Lane looked at Rob in surprise. But Rob resumed.

"You've sensed from your first encounter that the council has no patience for dissent, no toleration for anomalies. Toe the line, or you're the enemy. And because you sensed how dangerous that attitude is, how tyrannies destroy societies from within, you objected to it. In doing so, you became the enemy."

Lane looked down, nodding.

"So what are we going to do about it?" Rob asked in conclusion.

"We're going to execute your plan," Lane replied.

Rob smiled, nodding. He said, "On to COTA."

Indeed, the next weekend's race was at the Circuit of the Americas, or *COTA*, the road course outside Austin, Texas. Dani and Elena joined Marla on the trip to Austin later that week.

Elena planned to help Marla with her race team management at COTA. Dani had not one but two invites to COTA. Darnell asked Dani to join him, as he had done for the Las Vegas race two weeks earlier. But Rob also asked Dani's help with security issues. Rob wanted Dani's coding and electronics insight.

Lane didn't know how to feel about COTA. COTA would be his first road course race for his new team. COTA was a tremendously challenging layout. It was also a favorite for Lane and many other drivers not for its ease but for those challenges, including elevation changes and blind curves.

Ordinarily, Lane would have looked forward to the challenge. But COTA also presented just as many, if not more, opportunities for electronic mischief of the sort in which Doyle and the council might engage. COTA's road course layout complicated the usual race telemetry. Drivers, teams, and officials just had a harder time keeping track of cars and their progress across the expansive layout.

And so despite Lane's on-track progress over the prior races, and despite his love for COTA's driving challenges, Lane felt more trepidation than anticipation about the COTA race.

Rob's plan to entice and expose the council also concerned and distracted Lane, if Lane had been willing to admit it. But heeding Rob's advice, Lane put that plan out of his head until it was time to execute it. Until then, he would concentrate on the race.

Darnell's race garage was next to Lane's garage. As qualifying neared, Darnell turned aside from his team's preparations to chat with Lane in the back of the garages. Darnell and Lane went over and over every challenging turn and enticing straightaway of COTA's layout. It was their first time speaking so openly and in such detail together about what they had learned of a race track.

Lane welcomed Darnell's trust and confidence. Lane had noticed that the team's two veteran drivers tended not to engage Lane about racing details. Lane believed that they cared about his success, just as they cared for Darnell. But Lane suspected that they were deferring to his famous dad Blake for racing tips and advice. The veteran drivers didn't want to appear to interfere between Lane and Blake.

Lane understood their standoffishness. The trouble was, still fresh in his retirement, Blake had stepped back. He wasn't even attending these early season races. Lane and Blake had never talked a lot about racing, Blake because he didn't want to force Lane into the sport, and Lane because he held his dad in such awe.

The dynamic left Lane without a racing confidante, indeed without a mentor and hearing board. As Lane chatted with Darnell about mastering COTA's challenging layout, he realized that Darnell might serve Lane well in one of those roles, so important for a young racer's continued development.

Darnell had different reasons for consulting Lane. First, Darnell liked Lane, as most other drivers did.

Darnell also respected Lane's elite driving talent, even if Lane was a bare second-year Cup racer, like Darnell himself.

Darnell's dating relationship with Dani also encouraged Darnell to get to know Lane better than he had. Lane felt a little more like family than just a teammate.

But Darnell had one other reason to befriend and rely more on Lane than he had initially expected. Darnell realized how much Lane's addition to the race team intimidated him. Lane had in the fans' eyes supplanted Darnell as the team's up-and-coming young driver. Darnell hadn't known how to handle that change, except to befriend and learn from Lane, just as Lane wished to befriend and learn from Darnell.

Circumstances had thrown Darnell and Lane together. And they had decided to take on circumstances as friends rather than solely as teammates and competitors.

As Lane took the track for his qualifying warm-up lap, he kept Darnell's tips and advice in mind. And then he was off on his timed qualifying lap, racing by the seat of his pants.

Lane loved qualifying runs, especially at road courses like COTA. Qualifying on a road course felt to Lane like pure racing, car against the track, without the distractions of competition.

Lane managed to hit every mark on his qualifying run. His crew chief and engineer had once again given him a fast car. Lane's qualifying time stood as the best until the last few cars, which are usually the fastest cars in the field, able to take advantage of what other times showed was the best approach to the track.

Lane qualified fifth, by far his best qualifying result. Darnell was not far behind in ninth. Both were ecstatic at their results. Both relished the next day's Cup race.

Lane and his crew chief and race engineer conferred late into the evening about race strategy. Given the speed Lane's car had shown, they decided to forgo stage points in favor of shooting for a top five or top ten finish. They even agreed that they would gamble on a race win if the opportunity presented itself.

Elena and Dani watched Lane and Darnell race the next day, from one of the trackside suites their drivers' race team had arranged for sponsors. They cheered Lane and Darnell on as both drivers held their own in the top ten throughout the early stages of the race. Both drivers looked to run strong.

The third and final stage commenced with Lane on a different pit strategy than most of the other leaders. A yellow caution, a restart, a red flag for a wreck cleanup, and then another yellow caution after the restart further scrambled the leaders.

"They've got you lined up thirty-third, Bud, behind the No. 28 car," Lane's crew chief radioed Lane as cars emerged from pit road to join the pack behind the pace car.

"What?!" Lane replied in shock, adding, "I should be right with the race leaders."

"Agreed," the crew chief replied as calmly as he could muster, adding, "We're checking with race officials."

Lane held his position as the cars continued to follow the pace car around the course.

"Back to thirty-third behind the No. 28," the crew chief repeated, adding, "They say telemetry confirms it."

"But that's not possible," Lane nearly shouted back, adding, "I've been running with these cars the whole race."

"They're going to black flag you if you don't drop back this time around," the crew chief warned.

Dumbfounded, Lane pulled out of line, letting car after car pass him until he was all the way back near the end of the field. Lane watched as Darnell and their two veteran teammates passed him. Lane finally pulled in behind the No. 28 car. The pack tightened up as it neared the restart zone, and they were off.

Lane was so furious, at the unexplained telemetry putting him so far back, that he could hardly concentrate on the race. It was one of the few times in a race car that Lane nearly didn't care for the results. He forced himself to compete, although he had no stomach for it. He gained only a few positions by the race's end, finishing twenty-eighth among thirty-five remaining cars on track.

Lane stormed out of the race garage without speaking to anyone, after parking his car in the garage. Fortunately, Elena and Dani were nowhere in sight. Lane avoided Darnell in the next garage and instead headed straight for the motorhome for a shower and change of clothes.

Yet as Lane approached the motorhome, he saw outside it the familiar white sedan. And just as Lane reached the motorhome's door, the sedan's back door opened, and Doyle stepped out.

Lane paused with his hand on the motorhome's door handle.

"A little telemetry problem?" Doyle sneered.

Lane scowled. But instead of replying, he opened the motorhome door. Without looking at Doyle, he gave Doyle a jerk of his head indicating that Doyle should follow him into the motorhome. Doyle smiled as he mounted the steps behind Lane.

Once inside, Lane turned to Doyle and asked with another scowl, "What did you say?"

"So, you had a little telemetry problem?" Doyle repeated with the same sneer.

This time, though, Doyle added, "Do you think maybe it's time we had a little talk?"

"What's there to say?" Lane answered curtly, still scowling.

"Oh, I have plenty of ideas for how to help," Doyle replied.

"Like what?" Lane shot back.

"Maybe with a little cooperation from you," Doyle replied, "We'd find a way to get you across the finish line where you deserve."

Both Lane and Doyle turned their heads toward the door to the back of the motorhome, from which a sound had emerged. The door swung open to reveal Rob.

"Anything else you'd like to say for the record?" Rob asked Doyle.

As he spoke, Rob held his cellphone recorder toward Doyle, making it clear that he had recorded their interaction.

To Lane's surprise, Doyle smiled. Pulling his own cellphone from his pocket, he placed it on the table and gave it a tap. The cellphone's speaker played a recording of Lane offering to throw a race.

Lane glared at Doyle, saying, "That's not me. I've never said that to anyone. You've fabricated that recording."

"Anything else you'd like to say for the record?" Doyle repeated Rob's line with another sneer.

Doyle turned toward the motorhome's door. Halfway down the steps, he stopped, turned back to Lane and Rob, and with a wan smile offered, "Let me know if I can be of any help to either of you. Have a safe trip home."

8

"This can't go on," Lane said to Rob in frustration and discouragement after Doyle had left. He added, "You don't believe that was me on his recording, do you?"

"Of course not," Rob said reassuringly but, cupping his hand to his ear as if someone might be listening, added, "Let's talk in my car on the way to the airport."

Lane nodded. Accepting Rob's caution that Doyle might have planted a listening device in the motorhome, Lane showered, changed, and hurried out to join Rob in his nearby rental car.

As soon as Lane joined him, Rob reminded Lane, "I warned you that today's plan would only be a first iteration in a series of more-challenging events. I expected Doyle to have a response, even if it wasn't exactly that response."

"What do you make of it, then?" Lane asked as he settled in alongside Rob for the drive to the airport.

"I'm pleased, actually," Rob said.

Lane looked at Rob disbelievingly but asked, "How so?"

"Well," Rob replied, "First, he did as we predicted, even as we bid."

Lane gave Rob another puzzled look. So Rob explained, "He showed up, followed you into the motorhome at your suggestion, and repeated the bribe he'd made last week."

Lane nodded with a hint of satisfaction.

"We also made him play a card he may not have wanted to play," Rob added.

"You mean the faked recording?" Lane asked.

Rob nodded, saying, "That was a weak fallback, it seems to me. He probably planned to play that for you anyway, even if we hadn't laid the trap. And he's probably thinking right now that he made a tactical error in playing it for us. Now he's got to deal with both you and me, not just you."

Lane nodded. But Rob's comment reminded Lane of something he'd been meaning to ask Rob. Lane said, "Why has he been after me? Why is he after anyone? Why doesn't he just do his dirty deeds in the darkness?"

"Exactly," Rob replied, adding, "You've hit on his weakness. And it will be his undoing, if we do our work correctly."

Lane guessed, "You mean his desire not just to control people but to let them know that he's doing it?"

Rob smiled, nodded, and replied, "He'd be a much more difficult opponent without that defect, if he'd been content to remain in the shadows."

"Then why is he risking everything to gain that twisted satisfaction?" Lane asked the question he meant to ask in the first place.

"It's the nature of tyranny," Rob replied. He explained, "In a way, he can't help himself. All tyrants from the beginning of time up to the twentieth century's worst tyrannies, sacrificing tens of millions of their own citizens, have demanded worship, not just obedience."

Lane shook his head. He soon repeated, "I don't know how much longer this can go on. Can't we do something about it?"

"Oh, we are," Rob said. He added, "Dani's helping me lead a team of digital forensics and cyber security experts right now, the same team that's been following the other anomalies of which you've been the target."

"You mean not just today's so-called *telemetry* issue," Lane asked with relief, "But also the temperature gauge, pit-road penalty, and simulator data issues?"

"Of course," Rob answered. He turned his eyes briefly from the road to give Lane a glance and smile, adding, "You didn't think we were leaving you out there all alone, did you?"

"How long do you think it will take?" Lane asked.

"I don't know," Rob answered.

Lane thought for a moment before replying, "Well, we'd better resolve it by Darlington."

Rob gave Lane another sidelong glance, asking, "Why Darlington?"

"That's halfway through the season," Lane replied, adding, "The team owner says our sponsors will reassess then."

"Darlington it is, then," Rob replied, adding, "But we've got our work cut out for us, and we'll need your help."

"Like today?" Lane replied, reminding Rob of the plan they had just executed together.

"Like today," Rob agreed, adding with an earnest nod, "And thank you."

Rob paused, searching for what he wanted to say to Lane.

"You know, kid, you're every bit your father's equal," Rob finally said.

"Ha!" Lane replied, "I suppose only time will tell. Right now, I'm not feeling like anyone's equal."

Rob soon dropped Lane off at the airport terminal for private jets, where Lane would fly back from Austin to Charlotte on the team owner's private jet with the team's other three drivers. Darnell was the first to meet Lane at the terminal.

"Way to go, friend," Lane greeted Darnell, adding, "That was quite a race."

Darnell had earned his first top-ten finish of the season.

"Yeah," Darnell replied, "We really ground that one out. Glad for the team." Darnell paused before adding, "Tough day for you guys, huh?"

Lane shrugged, replying, "We actually ran great. That telemetry thing putting us at the back of the pack was just strange."

"Strange indeed," Darnell agreed. He added, "You alright?"

"Alright enough," Lane replied, concluding, "On to Richmond."

The next Cup race was indeed at Richmond Raceway's D-shaped three-quarter-mile track, just outside Richmond, Virginia. At about a five-hour drive from Charlotte's home for so many race teams, Richmond didn't require long-haul travel or even a plane flight. The race teams would have as much as an additional day to rest, recover, and prepare for the next Cup race.

Lane and Darnell had their usual duties, much of which involved simulator time to refresh themselves on Richmond's challenging layout.

Richmond's challenges are unlike any other Cup track. Richmond is the only three-quarter-mile track, a true *tweener* between the short half-mile tracks and the traditional mile-and-a-half tracks.

Cars at Richmond attain significant speeds. The top qualifying lap average speed is around 120 miles per hour, turns included. Straightaway speeds are much higher. Yet the track has little banking, no higher than fourteen degrees. The cars must find whatever little grip they can to navigate the big, swooping curves at the D-shaped oval's ends. And the track is very wide, making for many potential racing lines and lanes.

Lane and Darnell also spent their usual considerable time working with their crew chiefs and race engineers on their preferred car setups to best meet Richmond's challenges.

As good as his cars had handled at Las Vegas and COTA, and as much speed as his cars had shown, Lane had greater confidence than ever that his crew chief and race engineer would find a good Richmond setup, even though that setup would be completely different. Darnell, too, was confident in unloading strong at

Richmond and improving his car through practice and qualifying.

What differed during Richmond preparations was that Lane and Darnell spent more time together. For the first time, they conferred with one another, and even got their crew chiefs together, at the race facility to investigate setups. Because their driving styles differed, those setups would differ. But they were still learning from one another.

Lane and Darnell were also together for the first time at the customary Tuesday-evening gathering at Rob and Marla's house. Darnell accepted the invite to join Lane, Elena, and Dani there, with a meal that Rob and Marla provided.

Darnell and Dani especially enjoyed the meal. Darnell's presence delighted Dani who brightened the entire evening. Darnell's humor was also good levity for the group, all of whose members tended toward seriousness. And Lane and Elena took the opportunity to reflect their own relationship off the joy that Darnell and Dani obviously took in theirs. It was a good mix.

After the meal and dessert, though, Rob apologized when turning the conversation toward business.

"That's two weeks in a row, Mister," Marla chided Rob in mock humor, adding, "These business interruptions aren't going to become a habit, are they?"

Everyone laughed. Marla, of course, knew that Rob needed to prepare the group for what was to come at Richmond and after. Marla simply wanted to reflect that both she and Rob valued family time and wanted to continue to support it.

Rob began by sharing that the motorsport's leaders had invited the new tech company's council to the Richmond race, ostensibly to help the council learn more about the industry's goals, needs, and culture.

Rob took care in introducing the subject because to Rob's knowledge, only Lane, Elena, and Dani were aware of security concerns surrounding the council. Darnell had not been a part of their confidential discussions. Neither Lane nor Dani had burdened Darnell with the concern.

"So, you're bringing the bad guys in," Darnell joked in response to Rob's disclosure of the Richmond invite.

Everyone looked at Darnell with surprise. Rob was the first to say something.

"Why do you call them bad guys?" Rob asked.

"You're kidding, right?" Darnell asked. He explained, "They shut down podcasts, jettison sponsors, walk around like they own the place, and repeatedly screw over Lane. You think drivers don't notice?"

Lane smiled. Feeling vindicated, he offered Darnell a high five. Darnell shrugged, as if he was just saying the obvious.

"Inviting them to Richmond isn't going to go well," Darnell added, to drive his point home.

"What do you mean?" Rob asked.

"Well, they'd probably say that we just don't fit their algorithm," Darnell replied, adding, "And there's at least a few drivers and team members who are more than ready to show them that indeed we do not."

Everyone around the table looked at Rob. Rob considered Darnell's last response for another moment before speaking, more to the others around the table than to Darnell.

"Darnell is right," Rob began, "Which is why the motorsport's leaders have invited them to Richmond, to learn more about their fit or lack of fit, as well as to see what adjustments they're capable of making."

"Seems to me you're just letting the camel stick its nose into the tent," Darnell said matter of factly.

The others chuckled at Darnell's way of putting it.

"Maybe so," Rob replied, "To see exactly what kind of camel we have."

Darnell shrugged, saying, "Seems to me that leaders who don't know their own camel shouldn't be bringing it into the tent. Who's to say that they're not doing things a whole lot worse than just mucking things up around here?"

Rob raised his eyebrows, replying, "Well, they may just be doing a whole lot worse. Maybe that's what we'll find out at Richmond."

Darnell shook his head, replying, "No, I mean stuff you'd have to find out another way. They'd never show themselves directly to you."

Darnell paused. After looking around the table, he turned back to Rob, saying, "Look, I'm sorry for speaking out. What do you want us to do at Richmond with this council? They're already into everything we do, from car setups to driving to podcasting to marketing and sponsorships."

Rob raised his eyebrows again. Taking a deep breath, he replied, "Just be yourselves, and let me know anything you think worth reporting."

Darnell looked around the table again before replying to Rob, "I guess that's easy enough. Off to Richmond. I just hope you security guys are doing more than inviting the bad guys in for a dog-and-pony show."

Lane, Elena, and Dani smiled at Darnell's reference. Rob simply raised his eyebrows again, while taking a quick look at Marla. Marla raised her eyebrows back at Rob.

The gathering broke up shortly later. After Lane, Elena, Dani, and Darnell left, Marla said to Rob, "Looks like you've got someone around here who's willing to speak their mind frankly."

Rob gave Marla a rueful smile, replying, "And maybe that's a good thing."

Elena and Dani once again accompanied Lane and Darnell to Richmond, as they had to Las Vegas and Austin. Marla drove Elena and Dani up on Friday. Elena and Dani spent Friday and Saturday nights with Marla at her hotel room while remaining free during the days to tour the grounds, enjoy the town, and connect with Lane and Darnell when the drivers were free of pressing duties.

The two dating couples were beginning to find times, places, and events when driver and girlfriend could enjoy one another's presence and when the two couples could enjoy each other together.

They sometimes got to watch together the truck series race or the second-level race in which Blake and

Marla had a team. They'd cheer on drivers, point out funny or strange things happening on the track or pit road, and marvel at the drivers' skill or lack thereof. It was a bit of a busman's holiday but enjoyable nonetheless.

Other times, the couples, together or separately, would duck out for a bite to eat or a refreshing walk. And they had the drivers' motorhomes in which to relax for some quiet time together. Life on the road can be hard, but it can also be good. Lane and Elena, and Dani and Darnell, were learning how to make it better.

The council's presence at Richmond proved anticlimactic, at least from the community view. The techy dress, mannerism, and voicing of the many council members just seemed odd to the drivers, crew members, and others who met them and tried to relate to them. To the motorsports community, the interactions seemed artificial, inauthentic. Even the greetings were peculiar.

Darnell and his crew chief, for instance, greeted three council members who paid a visit to the race garage during a special time set aside for that purpose. The council members were there only to observe and interact with the crews, not for any technical work. And the crews were on alert to support that interaction, for the brief period the sport's leaders had arranged.

"Good to see you," Darnell had greeted the three council members as they entered his garage.

Darnell picked up a rage to wipe his right hand of garage grime before extending it for a handshake. The three council members looked at Darnell's hand as if covered with leprosy. None accepted the handshake.

"So how's it going?" Darnell had asked in a second try at cordiality. When his query brought no prompt response, he added, "Seeing anything interesting?"

The three council members looked at one another, shrugging.

"Guess not, then," Darnell answered his own question with a hint of sarcasm. He tried one more time, offering, "Any questions I can answer?"

One of the three council members gave a shake of the head. The three looked at one another, shrugged, and moved on to the next garage.

Darnell looked at his crew chief, asking, "Did you hear them say anything?"

"No," the crew chief replied, adding, "I think they're on a different frequency."

Darnell laughed. As he did so, he held up both hands, twisting imaginary dials and saying, "Driver to council. Driver to council. Do you read me?"

The crew chief laughed, saying, "Let's get back to work."

Other community reports getting back to Rob were the same. As one pit crew member put it, the council treated the visit as if the Richmond Raceway scene was their laboratory and the crew members their lab rats.

Rob heard of nothing nefarious, only a gross disparity in how each side viewed relationships. Stock-car racing was a family where community relationships were important, more important than anything else.

By contrast, the council members seemed to treat relationships as meaningless. The council members only seemed interested in what they could touch and measure, not what their absent emotions might have experienced or distant souls might have sensed.

Doyle, though, was different. Among the council members, only Doyle seemed at all interested in relationships. Doyle, at least, greeted others. He sometimes shook hands when offered. He sometimes listened and replied to offers and inquiries. And for the most part, he did so cordially.

The only thing that Rob heard about Doyle, which Rob had also sensed, was that Doyle seemed to calculate and manipulate his interactions. Doyle seemed to know with whom he should speak and with whom he need not do so. Doyle mostly ignored anyone whom he judged to be without power or influence.

In stock-car racing, the most powerful and influential tend to speak early and often with the least powerful and influential, extending rich kindness where they have nothing to gain. Doyle seemed ready only to do the opposite, to interact appropriately only out of obligation for personal or corporate gain.

In short, no one had a good thing to say about Doyle. And Rob was unable to repeat in polite company some of the bad things Rob heard said about him.

Lane also dutifully reported his own odd interaction with Doyle at the race garage. Not long after the council had paid its peculiar visit, Doyle had stopped by on his own, on the same arranged tour of the garage area. Lane, busily conferring with his crew chief in the back of the garage, had noticed Doyle standing outside the open door of the garage. Doyle appeared to wear his mischievous grin as he surveyed the busy garage.

Lane had ignored Doyle, hoping that Doyle hadn't even seen his glance and would simply pass on to other garages. But to Lane's disappointment, Doyle had called to Lane from outside the garage.

"Fixing all the problems?" Doyle had asked with that hint of sarcasm with which Doyle seemed always to speak.

Lane had avoided even looking toward Doyle. Hoping that Doyle would quickly pass on, Lane had replied with a quick and simple, "Yup."

"He's gone," the crew chief said a moment later, adding, "What was that all about?"

Lane shrugged, not wanting even to think about it at the moment. They had a race for which to prepare.

Rob, though, gained other important information during the course of the council's Richmond visit that he would use later in his investigation. For Rob, the visit was a resounding security success, even if it was a painfully useless exercise for the rest of the community.

The Cup race proved to be the exciting and challenging event that Lane had anticipated. Indeed, for Lane, the Cup race itself was likewise a resounding success. His car had both speed and handling, both requisites for Richmond success. His team's strategy was spot on. And for once, nothing during the race interrupted Lane's success. Lane finished third, his first official top-five finish for his new team.

Lane's pit crew greeted him royally as he steered his car back to the race garage. Darnell congratulated Lane outside their race garages as soon as they had both wiggled out of their cars.

Lane was, above all, elated. He had every reason to feel that things were turning the corner. But as he gathered himself in the motorhome for the drive home, the call from his crew chief came on his cellphone: their car had failed post-race inspection. Lane was disqualified. He had officially finished last.

As Lane listened to his crew chief's brief explanation of the disqualification, his cellphone signaled a text. Still listening to his crew chief, Lane glanced at the cellphone's screen. The text read simply, *Too bad. Time we talk?*

Lane didn't have to guess at the text's sender.

9

"Where did we fail?" Lane finally asked his crew chief over his cellphone, after the longest pause of stunned disbelief and discouragement.

With his heart pounding and his ears ringing from both the cellphone call and Doyle's gloating text message, Lane's voice sounded to himself like it was coming from the bottom of a well.

"I don't have the optical scanning station's readout in my hands yet," the crew chief began, "But it sounds like the body was out of manufacturer tolerance all along the profile."

"But that's impossible," Lane rejoined. He argued, "We passed pre-race inspection fine, and we didn't have any significant damage to the body in the race, not even any hard contact."

"Well," the crew chief surmised, "That's probably part of the problem. If we'd had some damage or even hard contact, they might have passed us through."

"Anything we can do?" Lane asked, already knowing the answer.

"I'll have a better answer for us once I see the scanning results and get to inspect the car," the crew chief replied. He added, "They're taking the car back to the Research and Development Center."

Lane didn't know what else to say. After a long silence, the crew chief said, "Let us get things packed up and get everybody back to the shop. We'll figure it out tomorrow."

"Yeah, thanks," Lane replied distantly. Without feeling the sentiment, he added lamely, "Tell the guys to drive safely and get some rest."

Lane sat down, listless and disconsolate. Every race so far that season had been a team disaster of one kind or another. They had been running so well in the last few races, with speed and handling, but had nothing to show for it. He was falling so far behind in the points standings already that his whole season looked to be lost.

Lane heard a light rap on the motorhome door. The door opened. Lane half expected to see Doyle's mischievous grin. Instead, Rob stood at the door, ready for their five-hour drive back to Charlotte together.

"You heard?" Lane asked without rising from his seat.

Rob nodded, saying, "Let's talk about it in the car."

Lane nodded, rose, grabbed his small bag, and headed out to Rob's car.

For the first hour, Rob made no effort to speak or get Lane to speak. They both needed to catch their breath, recover, and process the day's events. The miles passed in silence, other than small offers here and there of a snack, music change, or temperature adjustment.

For Lane, it felt good just to let the miles tick by, driving down the interstate. He recalled the sensations he had felt throughout the day's race, successful but for the post-race disqualification.

Lane loved to drive, especially to race. He had always loved to drive, for as long as he could remember. He had even loved to sit in a car seat in the back of his folks' van, with his famous race-driver dad Blake at the wheel. Lane remembered imagining, from his back-seat car seat, that his dad was racing them down the interstate, driving the whole family to another exciting win.

When Lane had taken the wheel of a go-kart at an early age, the driving bug had bitten even harder. To feel a vehicle's power and speed is one thing. To *control* it is another thing.

If Lane hadn't found a career as a race driver, he would have been happy driving a long-haul eighteen wheeler or even a delivery truck. Indeed, as the miles back to Charlotte ticked by, Lane remembered as a child envying the delivery drivers who rushed up to his house in their big, sleek vans, dropped off a package, and then rushed away.

Race driving added the element of competition. But Lane drove more for the experience of guiding the great race machines around their fabulous race tracks than for the wins and losses of competitions. Lane drove for that sense of extending his senses through the machine into the track surface and air around him.

Lane could remember being on hunts with his dad and friends, where they would sit silently in a blind for hours, until their senses could nearly feel the trees, twigs, air, and sounds around them. Race driving took something similar, that stilling of the mind to feel into the car and track around the driver.

Lane took a glance at Rob at the wheel of their car. Lane remembered Rob saying something like the creator blessing us with finitude to make his infinite nature complete.

Lane imagined the infinite, that great central animating figure of humankind, desiring humanity's limitedness. And Lane suddenly realized that race driving was his reach toward the infinite, desiring the creator's loving embrace.

Rob suddenly slowed the car, pointing ahead to several deer preparing their mad dash across the interstate. Lane nodded. The moment broke Lane's reverie, returning his thoughts to the day's events. He picked up his cellphone from the console, gave it a swipe to turn off the music, and set it aside.

"Do you think the council was responsible for the disqualification?" Lane asked calmly in the fresh silence.

Rob took a deep breath before replying, "I don't know. It's possible."

"How so?" Lane asked, thinking of the physical templates race officials used for the car inspections.

"Anything electronic is subject to interference," Rob replied. He added, "We'll be looking into it, but a signal or module could alter the input data into a failed readout."

Lane nodded, remembering that race officials used an optical scanner for post-race inspection. Because of the high likelihood of car damage during the race, officials didn't use the pre-race inspection's physical templates.

"Did you learn anything from the council's visit?" Lane asked, again with a calm that sounded to Rob almost like serenity.

Rob stole a sidelong glance at Lane, assessing yet again how much Lane could handle. Rob noticed that Lane had relaxed and to some extent recovered. The silent hour of driving, deep in thought, had done its work. Lane still looked to Rob like the kid he had watched grow up alongside his dad. But Rob knew he'd need Lane to know more of the investigation. And now seemed to be the opportune time.

"Yes," Rob replied, adding, "On a strictly confidential basis."

Lane looked at Rob who added, "That's right. What I'm about to say no one else hears until this whole thing is over."

Lane nodded. Rob nonetheless reinforced his caution, saying, "I'm only telling you because you'll soon need to know, if the investigation unfolds as I suspect it must."

Lane nodded again, this time raising his eyebrows to indicate to Rob that he understood the seriousness of the confidentiality concern. Rob stole another glance at Lane, confirming that Lane understood. Rob continued.

"Our digital forensics and cyber security team had federal law enforcement warrant authority to secure their electronic device information for electronic search purposes," Rob divulged.

"Like through wifi or bluetooth?" Lane asked.

"Not exactly that but like that," Rob agreed.

"So you'll finally be able to learn through their devices what they might be doing to affect race outcomes?" Lane asked.

"Maybe," Rob agreed, adding, "And not just race outcomes but other things."

"Like data sales to gamblers and marketers and things?" Lane asked.

Rob nodded, saying, "Maybe."

"Feels like it's about time," Lane replied.

"It's not that easy, these things," Rob replied. But taking another glance at Lane, Rob caught himself, adding, "Although it's a lot easier than what you've been going through."

"Thanks," Lane replied quietly.

"It just takes time," Rob corrected himself. He reminded Lane, "You've given us until Darlington, right?"

Lane smiled, nodding and saying, "Not like I have a right to give anyone deadlines."

Rob smiled back, saying, "I understand the sponsor pressure, believe me. Darlington's only a month away, so we're moving as fast as we can."

Rob paused before resuming. Raising his eyebrows to highlight the sensitivity of his next disclosure, Rob said, "Our tentative plan is for a Darlington surprise."

"Am I going to be in on the surprise?" Lane asked with a chuckle.

"You're going to be the surprise," Rob answered in dead seriousness.

Lane looked at Rob who kept his eyes on the road ahead but for a brief sidelong glance to assess Lane's reaction.

"Well," Lane answered with another chuckle, "This should be interesting."

"I'll have more for you soon," Rob replied. He reminded Lane, "Not a word to anyone. And you and I are only communicating about it in person when I'm sure our communications are secure. Got it?"

Lane nodded. Rob needn't have reminded him. But Rob's reminder gave Lane a thought.

"Can I just put the whole thing out of my head until Darlington?" Lane asked.

Rob considered for a moment before replying with a smile, "You know, that would be a good thing."

Lane smiled back. He picked up his cellphone from the console, gave it a swipe to resume the music, tipped his head back against the headrest, and closed his eyes. The rest of the trip concluded in blissful silence.

Darnell greeted Lane the next morning at the race facility with a plan. Darnell had arranged to rent a go-kart track the next evening. They'd invite as many young couples, including drivers, crew members, and their girlfriends or wives, as would join them. And they'd have some fun, ostensibly to prepare for the next weekend's bumping and banging at Martinsville Speedway's short track.

Lane was all in. They recruited Elena and Dani to help them organize the event and get out the invites. They also planned races for the wives and girlfriends, to get everyone involved in a night of fun.

The event proved to be the perfect introduction for Martinsville's short-track week. Everything about Martinsville, stock-car racing's shortest track, feels different. The close quarters of the track, known as the *paperclip* or *half mile of mayhem*, seem to reflect themselves across the community, drawing it closer than ever throughout the week. The track's proximity, just a little more than two hours away from the sport's Charlotte home, adds to the feel of a family reunion, where the participants both squabble and celebrate.

Darnell's comedic timing, planning a raucous night of go-kart racing, was its usual perfect. Without entirely intending it, Darnell had given Dani a sort of coming-out party, a true debutante's introduction to the motorsport's community. Because everyone credited Darnell with the event, they treated his new girlfriend Dani as the event's co-host, princess, and queen.

Throughout her upbringing, Dani had kept her distance from racing. Thus for Lane, seeing Dani take a leading role in the social life of his beloved racing community was a wonder and revelation. For the first time, Lane could imagine Darnell and Dani someday being the sport's ambassador couple, even though they were currently only new kids on the block.

Lane also saw Elena in another light. Elena had grown more and more comfortable as Dani's supportive sidekick. The two were learning how to amplify the best of one another. The go-kart event also gave Lane hints of how Elena could relate to the racing community, not as its ambassador but as a vital member with a unique background and deep insight.

Lane loved how Elena sparkled in Dani's presence, not from Elena's natural grace and beauty but from a joy beginning to radiate from deep within her. And at moments through the evening, Elena saw that Lane was seeing her in a joyful state, embraced by her still-new community.

Darnell's informal, spontaneous night of racing revelry thus watered the roots of both growing relationships, Darnell and Dani, and Lane and Elena. Their customary Tuesday evening with Rob and Marla would have to wait for next week.

Darnell's go-kart event also put Lane in an unusually good mood for the week. When he walked into the race facility the next morning to finalize race setup and strategy with his crew chief and race engineer, Lane greeted them with the quip, "Okay. For what disaster shall we plan this week?"

The crew chief and race engineer looked at one another briefly, wondering if Lane was serious. Then they all broke out laughing.

Lane and his crew chief had decided early in the week that they should change nothing in their approach to track setup and race strategy, other than to address the unique demands of Martinsville's paperclip race track. They'd had good track success. Indeed, if they could simply continue to repeat that success, they were confident that at some point, the disasters would end, and they'd soon have their first top fives and race wins.

At their final Wednesday morning meeting, they confirmed that they had no need to throw everything out to start over, or to throw a Hail Mary with a daring, throw-caution-to-the-wind setup and strategy.

"So, do you think Martinsville is going to be our race?" the crew chief asked Lane, after they and the race engineer had settled on the final setup and strategy.

Lane's answer surprised the crew chief and race engineer.

"Not really," Lane replied, adding, "I'm convinced that Darlington is going to be our turn. I'm expecting a Darlington dawn. Until then, we're just going to keep weathering the storms."

Lane gave them no reason for his answer. But he had clearly in mind that the council wasn't yet done with him. Indeed, the moment his crew chief had asked, Doyle's mischievous grin, standing outside the Richmond race garage, had appeared in his mind.

Later in the week, Darnell and Lane drove the two-plus hours to Martinsville together. On the way, they discussed car setup, short-track racing tactics, and anything else germane to their upcoming challenge. Lane had never spoken so frankly with another race driver. He was glad to have Darnell with whom to speak, sensing that bouncing ideas around with Darnell was helping him clarify, adjust, and confirm his own insights.

Lane found another opportunity that week for more insight. Lane was watching the second-level series cars practice, from a grandstand vantage point drivers and crews favored when not involved in the race, when the race official Fred walked up.

"How's it going?" Fred asked, taking a position beside Lane at the grandstand rail to watch the practice.

Lane shrugged, saying, "The driving's going great. The results not so much."

"Those tech demons are still giving you trouble, aren't they?" Fred observed matter of factly.

"Sure are," Lane agreed.

"When's it going to be over, do you think?" Fred asked.

"Darlington," Lane replied, without looking away from the practice on the track below.

"Sounds about right," Fred agreed.

Lane looked at Fred, asking, "Why?"

Fred had a glint in his eye, from which Lane wondered whether Rob had let Fred in on something. But Fred only answered, "Darlington is history. Darlington is home. Darlington is *us*, as much as or more than any other track. Darlington is where things get worked out, in the deep way that stock-car racing needs to work things out."

Fred paused. He asked Lane, "Feeling anxious?"

Lane thought for a moment before shaking his head.

"Good," Fred said, adding with a smile, "Anxiety is only a marker for the emergence of entropy, anyway. And despite your disappointing results, you're definitely keeping entropy under control."

Lane smiled and shook his head at Fred's clinical way of putting things. Then Lane had a thought he'd been meaning to ask Rob or Fred.

"Why are the council members so different?" Lane asked Fred.

"You mean our friends who visited us in Richmond last week?" Fred asked with a wry smile.

Lane nodded, saying, "But I haven't run into anyone who's called them friends."

"Do you want the short answer or the long answer?" Fred laughed.

"Give it your best shot," Lane laughed back.

Fred composed his thoughts for a moment. He then began, "Well, if you know the story all the way back, technology followed the fall, when we grasped for the opposition of good versus evil, against the creator's warning."

Lane screwed his face up in confusion. He knew the traditional story of humankind's paradise fall. He just hadn't thought of it as relating to technology. So Lane said simply, "Explain."

"Desiring to know both good and evil, rather than to receive their definition from the creator, is choosing opposition for an identity," Fred explained. He paused before adding, "Good and evil are diametrically opposed. Knowing both, in the sense of embracing and consuming both, which is what the original story portrayed and means, naturally produces a confused, fractured, conflicted identity."

Lane nodded, after a moment's thought to digest Fred's statement. Lane then asked, "But what's the relationship of this grasping fall, to technology and the council?"

"Banished by our self-selection from the paradise of knowing only good, we instantly need our own society and technology for survival," Fred offered. He added, "But cursed with having embraced both good and evil in diametric opposition, our technology will both do good for us and curse us."

"I think I need an example," Lane said lamely.

"Every technology is both an instrument of production and oppression," Fred ventured. "A knife cuts wood and meat but also threatens and kills a neighbor. A vehicle transports both the sick and the violent oppressor. We wage war with the same instruments, or at least the same technology, with which we make peace."

"That still doesn't get us to the council," Lane replied after another moment's thought.

"Oh, it does," Fred said, explaining, "The council, conceiving of itself as a pure and unadulterated tech representative, puts technology in the creator's place, when technology is neither good nor bad, only opposition of one with the other. Pure technology is soulless hell, not heart-filled heaven."

"They do seem like people without souls," Lane said. As he said so, though, Lane was thinking not so much of his odd encounters with the council members but of the joy he, Elena, Darnell, and Dani had shared at Darnell's go-kart event. But Lane had one last question for Fred.

"But we're all about technology, too, aren't we?" Lane asked, waving his hand at the cars whirling around Martinsville's short track below them.

"No," Fred replied, "We're about people."

"People?" Lane pressed Fred.

"Yes, people," Fred replied. He paused, then concluded, "Remember, we're about *stock* car racing, not just auto racing. That means we've always got an eye on the human proportion and humane soul of the sport."

Lane smiled. He liked that, not because it sounded good but because it was true. He now had a connection between the sport he loved and the people he loved.

10

"Got your back up here," Billy the spotter called in with his radio check to Lane from atop the grandstands, as the cars warmed their tires on Martinsville's short track far below, preparing for the race start. "Let's avoid the worst of the bumping and banging."

"Roger that," Lane replied from inside his car.

"Every lap counts, friend," Lane's crew chief chimed in, adding, "Give it your all."

"Will do," Lane replied over the radio, adding, "Thanks for a great car."

Lane's team had indeed given him a great car. He had qualified in the top ten, a big advantage at Martinsville, where passing can be difficult, and working one's way up through the pack even harder. He just needed a solid race without mishap, to build on the momentum their fast cars had been offering the team.

The pack assembled into its rows, two by two, with Lane in the fifth row. Through the starting zone they came, the leaders leaping forward. Lane feathered the gas perfectly, avoiding spinning his tires, while staying near the bumper of the car ahead of him. They flashed under the waving green flag. The half mile of mayhem had begun.

Lane completed the first lap in what seemed like an instant. Cup cars circle Martinsville's half mile in right around twenty seconds. Lane battled to hold his position for a second lap and then a third lap. The cars began to sort themselves out into the single file with which the race would begin, until the cars laid more rubber down and the lane options expanded.

Still battling on the outside row, Lane listened for Billy to tell him he was clear to drop down to the inside row, where the preferred line was forming. Nothing.

Lane pressed on for a fourth lap and then a fifth lap, whirling around and around the short track, looking for a chance to dive down to the inside lane. Cars were beginning to pick Lane off, one by one. He was already falling quickly back.

"Billy?" Lane radioed, "Give me a call. I need to get down."

Nothing. Lane realized he had lost radio contact.

Billy and the crew chief could hear one another. Billy had been coaching Lane through the first several laps, to no avail. Billy had called openings out to Lane down on the inside line, but Lane had ignored them for lap after lap, until Billy and the crew chief realized that Lane had lost radio contact, apparently at the instant of the race's start.

Drivers sometimes lose radio contact. Lost radio contact can involve headset failures, microphone issues, frequency issues, and any number of other things.

The options for restoring radio contact are not generally good. Making a headset swap would extend a pit stop well beyond any reasonable time. The only plausible fixes are remote, outside the car, such as frequency changes or swaps of the spotter and crew chief's equipment.

The options for working without radio are also not good, especially at a short track like Martinsville. Pit crews can hold a signboard aloft along pit road, indicating to the driver when to pit, presuming that the driver can pick out the sign board when flying by on the track in the midst of fierce racing competition.

As to track conditions, especially when the driver is clear to move up or down the track, the driver without a radio is on the driver's own. At a short track like Martinsville, forty competing cars pretty much mean a driver is always in or around traffic. Thus, being on one's own, without knowing when one is clear to change lanes, is a huge disadvantage.

Lane fought valiantly on without radio communications but inevitably fell further back. Lane could have pressed the issue. His car, once again fast and handling well, would have allowed him to make up lost ground. But Lane would soon have surely wrecked himself and other cars if he had taken the risks he would need to take while racing blindly, without a spotter.

Lane's gut, though, told him not to take the risks but to race safely, conservatively, hoping for the miracle of restored radio communications. The miracle never came. Lane finished the race laps down, way back in the pack.

The only miracle was that Lane finished the race at all. Without radio, Lane had to guess on so many things, not just lane changes but tires, gas, and pit strategy.

Missing radio communications certainly angered and frustrated Lane throughout the race. But as the race wore on, Lane had begun to think differently. He had to consider things he would not ordinarily have considered. And without listening to the radio and mentally processing frequent radio communications, Lane felt that his attention to the car and track were more acute than ever.

Lane realized late in the race and afterward that he had gained valuable experience. He had heard of drivers racing with lost radio communications. Now, Lane had experienced it. He certainly wouldn't have asked for it. But now that it had happened, Lane had a perspective on racing he would not otherwise have had. And just maybe, that perspective would soon make a positive difference.

Lane's team had begun diagnosing the issue from the moment they realized they had lost radio communications. They found nothing during the race. The problem wasn't with their equipment.

The diagnosis continued immediately after the race, when the team recovered Lane's helmet radio headset. Oddly, they found nothing to explain the radio failure, either. Lane's headset checked out fine. Indeed, once the race concluded, the headset appeared to be working as normal.

The inexplicable radio failure shocked the crew chief, race engineer, and rest of the team. It didn't shock Lane. He felt he knew the cause.

As Lane headed to the motorhome to shower and change for the drive home, he considered that Doyle might be outside the motorhome once again to confront him. And indeed, there outside the motorhome, was the familiar white sedan. Doyle emerged from the rear driver-side door as Lane approached.

"Difficult race," Doyle observed with a sympathetic shake of the head and strained smile.

Lane nodded without looking at Doyle, Lane focused instead on opening the motorhome door and getting inside.

"Mind if I join you for a chat?" Doyle called as Lane mounted the motorhome steps.

Lane shrugged. Doyle followed Lane up the steps.

Inside the motorhome, Lane tried to ignore Doyle. Lane instead gathered and put away his things, preparing to head to the back of the motorhome for his shower and change.

Doyle pressed on, saying with an exaggerated sympathy right out of central casting, "It's a shame. These difficulties have all been so unnecessary. If only you'd let us help, I'm sure we'd find a quick fix."

Lane paused from his manufactured busyness, saying, "I suspect your help comes at a cost."

"Oh yes, everything has a cost," Doyle replied, adding, "But our cost is not nearly as steep as what you've already endured."

Lane shook his head in a pitying manner.

Doyle again pressed on, saying, "If, hypothetically, I could guarantee you a late-season win, say in a Crown Jewel event, you'd surely be wise to consider it. It would represent an extraordinary success for such a young driver."

Lane nearly stole a glance at Doyle but resisted doing so. Lane recognized the attraction of what Doyle had suggested. If he engaged Doyle now, Doyle would rightly construe that he had dangled the right carrot.

Doyle again pressed on, adding, "And the only cost would be that you struggle valiantly on, *nearly* winning races."

Doyle smiled at the way he had put it.

Lane finally jumped in. He turned to Doyle, spelling it out matter of factly, "So your sportsbook client is making a killing by luring bettors into wagers on a certain popular young driver's win for his leading team. The better the young driver does, *without winning*, the more money your client makes on lost bets. Your client only needs to know when the young driver will finally win, by which point your client can adjust the odds for yet another big profit."

Doyle didn't miss a beat, replying with a sly grin, "Well, that would indeed be a profitable scheme, if one were to arrange it."

Lane, though, wasn't done. He resumed, this time angrily, "But that would only be the tip of the iceberg. Once you had control of the popular young driver, you'd have control of the sport. You could do as you pleased, knowing that even the young driver's own family members wouldn't risk rocking the boat against you."

"Now," Doyle replied, again with a sly smile and without missing a beat, "Wouldn't that be something, that the popular young driver would soon reach every goal for which he had set out, guaranteed of the results."

Lane finally looked straight at Doyle, saying, "I'm winning at Darlington, without your help. Now, get out."

Doyle raised his eyebrows, saying, "So, you think Darlington, do you? No, that's much too soon. If you had any sense, you'd know you don't stand a chance."

Doyle turned abruptly to the motorhome's door. But he stopped halfway down the steps, turning back to say, "Let's have another chat after Darlington. Maybe by then, you'll have learned who's in charge."

Lane simply shook his head as he turned to the back of the motorhome for his shower and change. A moment later, he heard the door slam. Glancing out the motorhome's window, Lane watched the white sedan drive off.

Lane rode home from Martinsville with Rob. Darnell, who had driven Lane to Martinsville, was driving Dani home. Marla and Elena had already left for home together.

On their way home together in the car, Lane asked Rob, "So how'd I do?"

"You mean in the motorhome?" Rob asked.

Lane nodded.

Rob replied, "Academy award."

Lane smiled. Lane knew that Rob had been listening and recording the exchange.

Lane had another question, though. He asked Rob point blank, "Was it the council?"

"You mean the radio failure?" Rob asked.

Lane again nodded.

"Probably," Rob said, adding, "Our team's already on it. We don't know how, yet, but anything electronic, they'd likely have the capability to interfere or find the capability if they desired to pursue it."

Lane shrugged, saying only, "On to Tallahassee."

"And soon, to Darlington," Rob replied. He added, "Will you and your team be ready?"

Lane nodded, replying, "We'll be ready. It's the one thing I can control."

That was Lane's message the next morning at the race facility and throughout the week leading up to Tallahassee: everything is about being ready for the next race, improving on whatever they had learned from the prior race.

"Ignore Martinsville," Lane urged his crew chief and race engineer as they sat in Lane's office, discussing the upcoming week's Tallahassee preparations.

"Ignore everything that doesn't make us better," Lane added. He continued, "We're on a mission. We may not win at Tallahassee or even Dover or Kansas in the following two weeks. But by Darlington, we're going to be winners."

The crew chief and race engineer looked briefly at one another, wondering what had gotten into Lane. They had expected Lane to be frustrated, disconsolate, and in need of encouragement. Instead, Lane was encouraging them. Lane was leading. Lane was taking charge of his team.

Each team owner has a subtle, and sometimes not-so-subtle, way of establishing who leads each race team within the owner's racing organization. At some teams, the crew chiefs call the shots on car setup and race strategy, and the drivers must follow along, like it or not. At other teams, the drivers call the shots on car setup and race strategy. The crew chiefs are there to serve the drivers.

Lane's team owner had been a driver and thus tended to give the drivers the lead in determining how their individual race team would perform. If the driver had the confidence and insight to call for certain setups or strategies, then the crew chief should generally do as the driver preferred.

But Lane's team owner also wanted each team to work together. The owner wasn't the sort to tolerate conflicts, disagreements, or strained relationships within the team. And the owner was willing to hold the driver accountable for good team relationships.

Lane could thus call his own shots on car setup and race strategy. Yet he had to do so with a substantial degree of respect, and at least some deference, to his crew chief and race engineer. If his crew chief and race engineer put up a stink, the trouble would fall on Lane, not them.

Lane's crew chief was glad to see Lane confident to lead the team. Yet the crew chief was by far the most experienced member of the team. And he was prepared not only to tell Lane but to take it to the team owner, if he disagreed with Lane's preferences on car setup and race strategy.

Lane and the crew chief hadn't disagreed on car setups yet. Indeed, Lane asked that morning that the crew chief and race engineer work on a setup for Tallahassee that would make Lane's car effective at pushing another one of the team's cars. The crew chief and race engineer were glad to do so. Darlington was coming up soon, the hardest track for setups. If they were going to disagree, it would be about Darlington, not Tallahassee.

Lane, Elena, Dani, and Darnell gathered once again at Rob and Marla's home Tuesday evening. Over dinner, no one talked about racing. They reminisced instead about Darnell's go-kart event the prior week.

Rob and Marla hadn't yet heard much about the event. The stories with which Dani and Elena regaled the group over dinner delighted Rob and Marla. Just as Lane had reflected after the event on how much Dani and Elena had grown in their roles within the racing community, Rob and Marla marveled over the same thoughts.

Elena, Rob and Marla could see, was blossoming into a confident, balanced, and even joyful soul. Elena had of course benefited from residing with Rob and Marla while working with Marla on race team matters. But Elena had clearly benefited even more from her growing friendship with Dani.

Rob and Marla could also see Dani blossoming through her relationship with Darnell. That relationship had given Dani a standing within the racing community apart from her famous dad Blake. Dani hadn't shown significant interest in the racing community, as Blake's daughter. But Dani was clearly relishing her racing-community role as Darnell's girlfriend.

After dinner, Dani, Elena, and Marla continued to chat over coffee at the kitchen table, while Rob, Lane, and Darnell moved to the den. Lane was the one, this time, who had some business to which to attend.

"How would you like to win at Tallahassee?" Lane asked Darnell.

Darnell laughed, replying, "What? Are you a magician or something? Because that's what it would take to guarantee a Tallahassee outcome."

Lane smiled. Darnell thought for another moment before adding, "How would *you* like to win at Tallahassee?"

"No thanks," Lane promptly replied, matter of factly.

Lane's response took Darnell aback. He replied, "What do you mean, *no thanks*?"

"No thanks," Lane replied again in the same calm, matter-of-fact manner.

Darnell looked at Lane who looked back. Lane then explained, "But I'd gladly push you to the win."

Darnell shook his head, saying, "Well, of course, as teammates, we'd help one another. That's our plan, isn't it? The four of us are going to run the whole race together, pit stops and everything, as far as we are able, right up until the end. But then, it's sort of *every man for himself*, isn't it?"

"Not for me," Lane replied. He added, "I'm offering to push you to the win, if I have any chance of doing so."

Darnell looked again at Lane, who for the moment seemed intentionally inscrutable.

"Well go ahead then, partner," Darnell replied with a laugh. He added, "I gladly accept your offer, even if I don't entirely understand it."

Lane leaned forward in his comfortable leather den seat, offering Darnell a high five to confirm their agreement. Darnell stood, stretched, yawned, and finally gave Lane a high five.

"I promised to get Dani home early," Darnell said, excusing himself from the room. He added, "Get some rest, friends. Tallahassee's going to be its usual wild self."

Darnell stopped in the doorway to the den, turned, and, with his brow firmly knit in doubt, asked Lane one more time, "Are you serious? Push me to the win?"

Lane smiled and nodded. Darnell shook his head, gave a dismissive wave of his hand toward Lane as if Lane had gone crazy, and left. Lane and Rob laughed.

After they heard Darnell and Dani leave, Rob asked Lane, "What was that all about?"

"Our plan is still for Darlington, right?" Lane asked Rob in reply.

Rob nodded.

"Well," Lane continued, "I'm sure the council isn't going to let me win until after we've executed our plan. If I can't win, I may as well help Darnell win."

"Sounds like a good plan," Rob replied with a smile.

11

"Go! Go! Go!" Elena and Dani cheered Lane and Darnell on, from atop Lane's pit box, as the last laps of the Tallahassee race unfolded.

Elena and Dani had gladly accepted Lane's offer to watch the race from atop his pit box. The racing community would gladly recognize, as appropriate, that Lane would have his girlfriend Elena and sister Dani atop his pit box. Family and intimate friends have that place and privilege.

Darnell might have extended the same offer to Dani. But his doing so would have been premature, a hasty step that could reduce the standing of both Darnell and Dani, separate and apart, in the eyes of the racing community.

And besides, Elena and Dani wanted to watch the race together, as had become their custom. Together, they could root one another's boyfriends on, celebrating their connections, even while their boyfriends competed out on the track, with tempered degrees of fury.

Tallahassee was the perfect race for Elena and Dani to watch together from atop Lane's pit box. Lane, Darnell, and their two veteran teammates would pit together, to get back on track together in the necessary train. Lane, Darnell, and their two teammates would also race together when possible, to ensure a line of cars from which to draft.

Lane's commitment to help Darnell throughout the race just made the race all the more satisfying and exciting for Elena and Dani to watch together. Lane had tied his fate to Darnell, whose fate was largely in Lane's hands. Few drivers win at Tallahassee without a committed racing partner. That's the nature of a superspeedway race, where all cars, with their reduced power packages, depend on the draft.

Lane had tailed and pushed Darnell throughout the race. As it turned out, with their cars set up for one another, Lane to push and Darnell to receive a push, they turned out to be great racing partners. With Lane's full commitment to Darnell's success, Darnell was able to lead them toward the front of the pack and to stay there throughout most of the race, save for a couple of necessary pit stops.

The last few laps of any superspeedway race are breathless excitement. This Tallahassee race was no exception. Elena and Dani repeatedly held their breath as Lane pushed Darnell around the great banked curves, at times into the lead. Then they would briefly fall back, only for Lane to push Darnell to the lead once again.

Lane and Darnell were very close to controlling the race. Only a couple of other cars and tandems appeared to have roughly equal control of their strategy and the race. And when the inevitable big wreck happened, as it does in most any superspeedway race's last few laps, Lane and Darnell were out front enough to avoid it.

Elena and Dani stood atop the back row of Lane's pit box for the race's final restart, after the lengthy cleanup of the big wreck. The race would end with a green-white-checkered finish, a two-lap sprint to the finish.

Darnell restarted in the outside or top lane, in the second row, with Lane right behind him. Once the green flag flew with the pack once again at full speed, the leader ahead of Darnell gained enough momentum to dive down in front of the bottom lane. The move left Darnell at the head of the outside or top lane, although two to three cars behind the leaders in the inside lane.

For the rest of that green-flag lap, though, Lane was able to push Darnell slowly forward, gaining inch by inch on the inside row. By the time the leaders reached the start/finish line again for the last-lap white flag, Darnell was at the rear quarter panel of the lead car on the inside lane.

In a risky move, Darnell inched lower on the big banked curve, to side draft off the leader's rear quarter panel. Lane inched lower with Darnell, to remain squarely on Darnell's bumper.

The move worked. Coming off the turn, Darnell inched ahead of the leader, with Lane still right behind Darnell's bumper.

If Lane hadn't been Darnell's teammate and hadn't been so committed to Darnell's success, things would at this moment have gotten dicey. Lane might have eased back to stall Darnell out, using the opportunity to gain momentum for a run past Darnell for the win. But any such tactic would at the same time have opened a window for another driver and car to win.

Instead, Lane stuck firmly and squarely to Darnell's bumper, down the backstretch and around the final curve. The car at the head of the inside lane tried to side draft Darnell but had fallen too far back. The same car managed to side draft Lane behind Darnell, slightly slowing Lane and thus reducing Darnell's push.

But it was too late. Darnell flashed under the checkered flag in the lead. Darnell won the race by a half a car length. The car on the inside lane took second, with Lane taking third, still behind Darnell on the outside lane.

Dani and Elena jumped, yelled, wept, and embraced in celebration atop Lane's pit box. Darnell had won a superspeedway race in only his second year with the team. He would almost surely qualify for the championship playoffs later in the year. Darnell was on his way to a great year.

Lane brought his car down pit road while Darnell did the celebratory burnout on the track. Lane paused as he pulled off pit road and toward the race garage, looking for Elena. Elena caught Lane's attention, rushing to the window of his car for a quick through-the-window embrace.

Dani waited at Lane's pit box for Darnell to bring his car slowly down pit road, accepting congratulations all the way. Darnell brought his car to a halt when he reached Dani so that Dani could reach in through the window for a quick congratulatory kiss. And then, Darnell rolled the car off to victory lane for a good half hour of celebration with team photographs.

Lane parked his car at the race garage to spend a while debriefing with his crew chief and celebrating with his pit crew. It had been a spectacular day, even if Lane hadn't won.

Soon, Lane made his way to the motorhome to shower and change. As he approached the motorhome, he examined the grounds for any sign of Doyle's white sedan. Seeing none, Lane breathed a sigh of relief. Banishing the thought of Doyle from his mind, Lane mounted the motorhome's steps.

Lane's cellphone buzzed with a text, just as he collapsed on one of the soft seats inside for a moment's rest, before getting ready to head to the airport with Rob for the return flight to Charlotte. Lane reached for the cellphone on the motorhome's counter. The screen showed a text from Doyle reading, *See how easy with a little help from a friend?*

Lane tossed the cellphone aside on the seat next to him, rose wearily, and headed to the back of the motorhome for his shower and change.

Lane was soon ready to head to the airport to catch the team owner's private jet back to Charlotte with the team's other drivers, including the still-celebrating Darnell. When Lane noticed Rob's vehicle pull up outside the motorhome, he grabbed his gear bag and quickly descended the motorhome steps to join Rob. Running around the vehicle to the passenger side, Lane opened the front door and jumped in the seat. Rob greeted him with a hearty smile.

Lane, though, noticed a figure behind Rob in the back seat. It was the team owner. Lane gave him a broad smile, reaching his right hand into the back seat for a quick handshake.

"Congratulations, Big Guy," the team owner said kindly to Lane.

"You, too," Lane replied, adding, "A win and a third place is quite a team showing."

The owner nodded. Rob interjected, "I'm dropping you both off at the private jet terminal and then running back for Marla and the girls. Our flight won't be for a while."

"Darnell?" Lane asked Rob.

"He's got the other two drivers," Rob replied, adding, "They'll meet you there soon."

The three occupants settled back for the airport drive. Soon, the team owner asked Lane to tell him about the race. Lane shared a few highlights with the team owner, unsure of what the owner wanted to hear.

"I think you're leaving out something important," the owner said when Lane had finished.

Lane looked back over his shoulder at the owner's expression, trying to anticipate the owner's query. But Lane found no clue in the owner's kind expression.

"Tell me about your decision to push Darnell to the win," the owner finally said without changing his kind expression.

Indeed, Lane hadn't mentioned his race strategy *not* to win. Lane hadn't mentioned that he and his crew chief and race engineer had deliberately set up their car to push, while encouraging Darnell's team to set up their car to receive the push. Lane hadn't shared that he had told Darnell of his intention, assuring that he and Darnell would work together throughout the race right up to its very end.

Lane hadn't said anything about his race strategy because he didn't know how the owner would regard it. Lane assumed that the owner would appreciate winning the race, even if doing so required that one of his four drivers, Lane, sacrifice his own chance to win.

But Lane wasn't sure. Perhaps the owner would see Lane's willingness to sacrifice a chance to win as a fatal flaw in Lane's race-driver makeup. And Lane didn't want to spoil the glow of the successful race with any mention of his struggle with the council and his gamble that the council would not have let him win in any case.

So Lane did what he had learned to do when unsure of his questioner's motivation. Lane asked the team owner a question he knew that he would want someday to ask, in any case.

"Did I do the right thing?" Lane asked, looking over his shoulder at the team owner.

The team owner finally broke his kind expression with a kinder smile. The owner nodded, saying only, "Under the circumstances."

Lane thought for a moment about the owner's reply before asking a second question.

"So it's not a team rule to always sacrifice for a teammate's win?"

The owner gave Lane another kind smile, this time shaking his head while saying, "Depends on the circumstances."

Rob drove on in silence for a couple of minutes.

The team owner soon continued, saying, "Your circumstances included some unique factors, Son."

Lane nearly blushed with the owner's kindness in referring to Lane as *son*. The same appellation from another person might have been an insult. From the team owner, it was instead a tender and heartfelt honorific.

The team owner resumed, saying, "You pushed your sister's new boyfriend and your own growing friend to his first Cup win. That was a unique opportunity."

Lane nodded. But the team owner wasn't done.

"You also continued your string of strong runs," the owner began, while to Lane's surprise adding, "Without challenging your nemesis council to steal a win or strong finish from you."

Lane hadn't known what the team owner knew or thought of the issues Lane continued to face with Doyle and the council. The owner's disclosure that he was aware of Lane's persisting conflict with the council was a huge relief to Lane. Lane was learning to assume that the team owner knew everything.

The team owner interrupted Lane's thoughts with another encouraging word, saying with the same kind smile, "You've got your father's wisdom."

This time, Lane blushed.

To relieve Lane of his embarrassment, the team owner turned the conversation to Rob, saying, "What do you make, Philosopher, of a race driver who sacrifices a win for a teammate's win?"

Rob chuckled at the owner's reference to him as a *philosopher*. After a moment's thought, though, Rob began with the assertion, "Race driving is highly ritualized behavior."

The team owner smiled in the back seat, relishing Rob's coming lecture.

"A ritual is simply any recognizable, repeated, ordered behavior that others recognize as appropriate to the context," Rob continued, adding, "Even animals engage in rituals."

Rob paused, waiting to see if his two listeners had discerned how his premise would answer the question of why sacrifice for a teammate's win. They had not.

Clueless, but eager to learn the connection, Lane asked, "What purpose do rituals serve, whether in racing or among animals?"

Rob smiled, sensing that Lane was on the right path.

"Rituals both reduce the cost of interactions and promote their goals," Rob resumed.

"An example?" Lane asked, noticing that the team owner was thoroughly enjoying their exchange from the back seat.

"Well," Rob replied, "Among animals, a dominance move that the weaker competitor accepts in lieu of a full fight might spare the weaker competitor's life. That's a cost saving for both the dominant and subordinate competitors."

"Was I the weaker competitor, then?" Lane asked with a slight note of offense.

Rob smiled, saying only, "Maybe, if disabled by the council, but that's not my point."

"What's your point, then?" Lane asked, ready for Rob to solve his own riddle.

"Racing is not a complete competition, not a pure fight-to-the-death fight," Rob replied, adding, "If it were, it would have far too high of a cost."

"You mean like a big superspeedway wreck every week?" Lane asked with a chuckle.

"Pretty much so, right," Rob replied. He continued, "All races involve some degree of ritualistic accommodation."

"You mean give and take?" Lane asked.

"Not necessarily give and take or compromise," Rob replied, adding, "Some drivers do all or most of the giving, while other drivers may seldom if ever compromise. But the sport still fills itself with rituals. Pushing a competitor to a superspeedway win is one of them."

"Thanks, Philosopher," Lane said somewhat sarcastically and with a note of disappointment, adding, "Any last thoughts?"

"Yes," Rob replied with a smile. He concluded, "Rituals bind us together as a community. The higher the offer the ritual addresses, the greater the ritual brings us together."

Rob paused, stealing a glance at Lane from the road. The team owner's smile widened in the backseat, anticipating Rob's last thought.

"You not only did Darnell a great favor today," Rob said to Lane, "But you did us all as a community a greater favor. You gave of yourself the greatest thing a race driver could give, making a winner out of a driver who without your last-lap pushing would have been a sitting duck."

The team owner chuckled, saying from the back seat, "Darn right."

Lane gave a small, satisfied smile. Seeing that Rob had concluded, though, he asked Rob a question he'd been wanting to ask.

"Did the council help me somehow during the race?" Lane asked, explaining, "Doyle texted me after the race suggesting as much."

Rob glanced in the rear view mirror at the team owner in the back seat. After a moment's thought, Rob answered, "Yes."

Lane raised his eyebrows in surprise. He hadn't heard or seen anything during the race to make him think the council had been involved. Rob explained.

"Coming off pit road the last time, race officials clocked you for speeding. But the council representative up in the booth said it might be a network transmission issue, so they called it off until they could make a post-race review."

Lane shook his head. A pass-through penalty for speeding would have set him way back. Without drafting help, he would have been effectively out of the race. Doyle had wanted him to run strong, just not to win. So Doyle had put a pit-road speeding penalty in his back pocket just in case.

Lane stole a glance into the back seat at the team owner.

Catching Lane's glance, the owner gave a dismissive wave of his hand, saying, "You two will get this council thing worked out soon, I'm sure."

The owner paused, adding, "Darlington's coming up. It would be good to have it over then, if you know what I mean."

The owner smiled and winked. Lane nodded. Rob gave Lane a sidelong glance from the road. Catching Rob's glance, Lane took a deep breath, shook his head, and muttered to Rob, "Our little plan sure better work."

Rob smiled at Lane confidently.

12

"Well, that's a good start on the Monster Mile," Lane's crew chief said.

The crew chief, Lane, and the race engineer had just finished their long strategy meeting at the race facility the next morning after Darnell's Tallahassee win. They were already preparing for the next weekend's race at Dover Motor Speedway's mile-long track. The track bears its infamous *Monster Mile* moniker due to its high banking and narrow straightaways. The way the track's unusual concrete surface eats tires adds to the track's notoriety.

The race engineer added, "Let's join the party."

True to his fun-loving nature and party-going reputation, Darnell had invited everyone to an afternoon-long victory party at the race facility. The organization would have celebrated without Darnell having spearheaded the effort. But this celebration was going to be more than the typical corporate affair.

Tallahassee had exhausted Darnell, but not so much that he wasn't up to planning a little more fun than the organization's office staff ordinarily would have.

While Lane was hard at work with his crew chief and race engineer preparing for Dover, Darnell enlisted Dani and Elena to help him retain three local bands. Each band would play for a part of the afternoon. And each successive band would be a little louder and more raucous, as the afternoon wore on and the refreshments flowed.

Darnell had to do some negotiating with the crew chiefs and facility manager, but he managed to commandeer the largest room in the facility, which just happened to be the vehicle-assembly room. Darnell's mechanics and pit crew members helped clear the center of the room, set up a makeshift stage for the band, and place tables and chairs throughout the room. They also made sure to clear a dance floor in front of the band.

By noon, they had stocked food and drink stations around the big room. The first band was setting up for sound checking. And curious personnel were beginning to congregate and chat. An hour later, the first band was well into its set, dozens of personnel were eating and drinking, and the room had filled. Another hour later, the second band had taken the impromptu stage, and the party was fully on.

For Lane, Darnell's party was a strangely enjoyable revelation. Like any race driver, Lane loved the assembly room for its sleek vehicles sparkling under the room's bright lights. The assembly room at all times featured at least four complete or near-complete vehicles, one for each of the organization's four race teams. Often, the room held twice as many race cars, one for the coming race and a second for the race to follow.

The fantastic-looking cars, with their exquisite paint schemes, were still in place during Darnell's party. The people, music, food, and drink flowed around and over the cars. It seemed to Lane as if the cars shared in the celebration.

Lane's other revelation had to do with Elena and Dani. Just as the two friends had lit and adorned Darnell's go-kart event, Dani and Elena were once again a focal point for the party.

Darnell's party was a workplace event, during working hours. No one else had the occasion to bring a wife or girlfriend. But Dani and Elena had helped Darnell organize the event. And Dani and Elena were the girlfriends of the two drivers, Darnell and Lane, who had together pulled off the Tallahassee win. In short, Dani and Elena had every right to be the belles of Darnell's ball. Belles Dani and Elena indeed were, circulating about the room together, engaging everyone in the festivities and fun.

But every belle needs a dance at the ball. And by the time the third band took the stage and got deep into its set, the dancing was on, first Darnell and Dani, then joined by Lane and Elena, then joined by anyone who had a little too much to drink or not enough.

The dance of the two young drivers and their beautiful girlfriends was more than a celebration of one of the two young driver's first Cup win. Their dance was a pinnacle, ritual, and representation. Their dance, though free form, fluid, and energetic, had a liturgical cast.

Surrounded by the observant race cars, equipment, crews, and staff, the dance lifted eyes and hearts to the sport's highest yearnings, reached only by a mysterious marriage of the male striving with the female potential.

Some wrongly assume that identity is a matter of labels, like the uniforms race drivers wear, emblazoned with sponsor logos. But identity instead involves layers of participation. The dance of the two beautiful young couples drew the mechanics, pit crew members, and office staff into participation, both figuratively in their souls and in some cases literally in their bodies and limbs. And as it did so, the dance of the two beautiful young couples elevated the community's whole.

The band and dancing concluded by quitting time around five or six o'clock. Crew chiefs and race engineers had already drifted off, as had administrators and other office staff. Pit crew members, still weary from the Tallahassee travel, headed home. Dani and Elena left, after custodial staff insisted that they not do any cleanup.

Darnell and Lane remained, sitting and chatting with the shop mechanics and other facility personnel who lingered, those who didn't travel with the team and had fewer chances to share in any celebrations.

Only then did Darnell and Lane see the team owner walk through, quietly greeting the shop mechanics. Darnell and Lane rose from their seats when the owner walked over.

"Memorable day," the owner observed to both of them. Lane and Darnell both nodded, too satiated to speak.

"I almost like these celebrations more than the victory lane celebrations at the track," the owner added.

Lane and Darnell nodded again, although neither would have quite shared the same sentiment.

"Thanks for making it a good day," the owner said to both of them with a smile. He added with a deep breath and slight yawn, "Time for me to head home to hit the hay."

Lane and Darnell smiled. Looking at one another, they quietly agreed that they were ready to head home, too.

For Lane, the upcoming race at Dover Motor Speedway meant another opportunity to hone his team's efforts for the climactic race two weeks away at Darlington. Lane didn't want a lull or letdown in the two weeks between Tallahassee and Darlington, weeks the Cup series would spend at Dover and Kansas. Lane wanted to keep the team's momentum strong. Momentum, though, has its own pendulum. Sometimes momentum swings this way, and sometimes it swings that way.

Dover strategy wouldn't involve pack racing, pushing, or aerodynamics. As a one-mile track, Dover didn't have the reduced-power package of the two-and-a-half mile superspeedways or even the significant aerodynamic issues of the traditional mile-and-a-half tracks. Nor did Dover have the bumping and banging of the true short tracks like Bristol and Martinsville.

While Dover calls itself the Monster Mile, the track doesn't intimidate drivers like a superspeedway, with all the uncertainty and the huge wrecks, nor frustrate drivers like a short track, with the constant battling just for minimal room to navigate around the track. Success at Dover doesn't depend on a friend to push, like a superspeedway, or avoiding making enemies, as at a short track. Dover can thus be a favorite track, rewarding smart, skilled, independent driving.

Lane looked forward to Dover, except for his now-constant concern surrounding the council's intentions. The council was no longer a mystery or specter. Doyle was no longer an enigma. The presence of Doyle and the council felt as real and consequential as any of the other things with which Lane had to deal, like car setup and race strategy. Except Lane had no control over or influence with the council.

For the briefest of moments, Lane thought of reaching out to Doyle for a truce or accommodation. The council seemed to have settled into the sport as deeply as its other institutions. Sure, drivers and others didn't think much of the council's members and even the council's actions and influence on the sport. But at times, drivers also didn't think much of the sport's rules makers, officials, or even its tracks. Maybe the council was just another reality with which Lane needed to deal.

But then Lane recalled Doyle's deceptions and manipulations, revealing the depths to which the council would go for obedience, obeisance, and control. The council was an opponent with which one could not negotiate. Negotiate with a tyrant, and you'll lose your soul.

Lane thus soldiered on. He put in his hours on the simulator, set up for Dover. He strategized with his crew chief and race engineer, going over the innumerable options for short-run speed, long-run speed, balance, tire strategy, pit strategy, points strategy, and race tactics and goals.

Even as he did so, though, Lane felt like Dover was a tune up for something bigger, just as Kansas would feel the following weekend. And that bigger thing was the bold plan Lane and Rob had for Darlington.

Lane's race team unloaded a fast car for Dover. Lane qualified in the top ten, continuing to show the speed that his team had coaxed out of the car in the several prior races.

Lane met Darnell at their race garages, late the day before the Cup race.

"How are you feeling about tomorrow's race?" Darnell asked.

"Good," Lane replied noncommittally, adding, "You?"

"Same," Darnell replied with equal noncommittal.

Both young drivers sensed that Dover would tell its own story, over which they might just have less influence than they hoped. Some races feel like that. Some races make a driver feel like they were just along for the ride more so than driving for the win. Dover gave Lane and Darnell that sense, even before the race's start.

Darnell's new challenge involved driving off a win. Driving after a win can be the winning driver's hardest challenge. A win certifies success. But success tends to remove the drive for achieving it. Darnell and his team didn't intend to let down. But intentions are sometimes not enough to fend off the deceptive comfort of success.

Starting in the top ten was a good break for Lane. Darnell, unfortunately, ran slow qualifying laps, leaving him to start nearer the back of the pack. Trying to race his way up through the pack gave Darnell an insurmountable challenge, especially with a car that lacked speed. He would finish the race no better than he started it.

Lane's race was more eventful than Darnell's day of slogging his way around in the middle of the field. Lane began the race strong. He gradually gained a few more positions through the first stage. Lane even neared the leaders as the stage end approached.

Yet as Lane got up on his wheel to race the last few laps for stage points, something peculiar happened with Lane's car. Lane pressed the accelerator to the floor out of each turn without the corresponding surge in power.

"What's up?" the crew chief radioed Lane, as Lane's car succumbed to other cars out of each turn.

"The engine's not responding," Lane complained, adding, "I'm mashing the accelerator with no engine response."

"Checking," the crew chief replied, as the race engineer studied the telemetry readouts.

With each corner exit, Lane lost more positions.

"Are you sure the pedal's going to the floor?" the crew chief radioed Lane.

"Positive," Lane replied, frustrated that the crew chief had even asked.

"Telemetry is showing only a three-quarter accelerator," the crew chief replied.

Lane rolled his eyes inside the car.

"It's not a mechanical issue with the pedal," Lane replied, adding, "The pedal feels fine."

"Engine electronics," the crew chief replied, adding, "Nothing much we can do trackside."

The stage ended with Lane well outside the top ten, earning Lane no stage points despite his strong run up until the stage's end.

Lane's crew chief decided not to open the hood or bring the car behind the wall for diagnostics on the ensuing pit stop. Doing so would lose so many positions as to likely bury Lane for the rest of the race.

Lane's car, though, sprang back to life on the restart. Just as he had during the first stage, Lane slowly gained track positions throughout the second stage. Nearing the end of stage two, Lane was once again solidly in the top ten, likely to earn stage points.

But the same engine issue Lane's car had experienced at the end of stage one repeated itself, as if on cue, nearing the end of stage two. As hard as Lane mashed the accelerator to the floor on corner exit, the engine just wouldn't respond. Lane fell well back out of the top ten, earning no stage points.

Lane's crew chief once again determined that Lane should race on, without opening the hood or bringing the car behind the wall.

Once again, Lane's car leapt back to life on the restart for the final stage. And once again, Lane gradually made his way forward through the pack, nearing the leaders toward the race's end. Yet as Lane pressed forward, trying to gain the last few places, the same engine issue arose, causing Lane to once again fall back by the end of the race.

The crew chief was waiting for Lane back at the race garage as Lane pulled the car off the track, onto pit road, and back to the garage.

"Probably a control module," the crew chief observed as Lane climbed from the car, throwing his gloves back in the car with disgust.

"Strange that a control module would only fail at the end of each stage," Lane replied before walking off, shaking his head. He didn't want to say or do anything to anger or aggravate his race team. His mood wasn't civil enough to remain.

Lane headed to the motorhome to shower and change. As Lane did so, he knew what to expect. The white sedan sat outside the motorhome. Doyle emerged right on time, as Lane approached. Lane opened the motorhome door and climbed in without a glance toward or word for Doyle. Lane just left the motorhome door open behind him for Doyle. Doyle followed Lane in.

"This is all such an unnecessary shame," Doyle commiserated in a grandiose manner. Doyle sat down in one of the motorhome's luxurious swivel seats, crossing his legs at ease.

Lane ignored Doyle as best he could, as he put things away and readied himself for a shower and change. Rob would once again be picking Lane up shortly for the drive to the airpark for the owner's private-jet flight back to Charlotte with the other drivers.

"Maybe it's time I shared something with you," Doyle resumed, adding, "Something that you might find more persuasive than these discouraging race losses."

Lane glanced in Doyle's direction. Catching Lane's glance, Doyle said, "Remember, I'm only trying to help."

Doyle breathed a deep sigh of mock sorrow, saying, "You see, our team has discovered some very discouraging information that we would much rather not bring forward."

Lane shook his head, already understanding the extortion in which Doyle was about to engage. But Doyle continued.

"You don't seem too concerned with your own advancement," Doyle acknowledged. He continued, "Yet your Tallahassee ploy suggests you may care more about others than for yourself."

Lane turned away, looking for a distraction. He moved to the refrigerator, pulling a water bottle from it and unscrewing its lid. Out of habit, he momentarily thought of offering a bottle to Doyle but immediately rejected the thought. Doyle resumed.

"It seems that key members of your organization, all the way to the top, aren't so discrete in how they misuse the internet's darker corners," Doyle said, adding, "What a shame it would be if that information came to light."

Lane turned to Doyle, saying, "I don't believe a word you say, buddy."

"Oh," Doyle replied, "You don't have to believe me. I may not be telling the truth at all. But you should now believe my willingness to proceed as I have indicated to you. You don't doubt my reach, do you?"

"No," Lane agreed, "I know you'd stop at nothing. No deception is too dark for you."

"Ah," Doyle replied, "So we do have a point of agreement. Perhaps that's all that we've needed from the start. I had wrongly assumed that you and I might agree on other points. But if we can at least agree on that point, then perhaps you're ready to reach an accommodation."

"I think it's time you leave," Lane answered. He could feel his blood rising with anger. But more than anything, he just felt overwhelming disgust.

Doyle rose to go. As he did so, he replied, "I hope you'll soon reconsider. You have such endearing friends and associates."

As Doyle eased himself down the motorhome's steps, Lane called behind him, "Let's talk after Darlington."

Doyle paused, turning back to study Lane.

"Darlington, eh?" Doyle said with a sly smile, adding, "Now that's such a quaint place. I do think it would bring back some important memories for you, of how you value your little racing community."

Doyle paused, then added with a leer, "Yes, let's speak after Darlington. And until then, I'd watch your step. Racing is a dangerous sport."

Doyle turned, descended the last step, and closed the motorhome door behind him. Lane watched through the motorhome's window as Doyle climbed in the back seat of the white sedan, and the white sedan motored off.

13

"Could the council manipulate the engine control module?" Lane asked Rob on the way to the airport.

Rob had already met with Lane's crew chief to review from a security standpoint the strange issue that had crippled Lane's race.

Rob shook his head at Lane's question, saying, "Remember?"

"Oh, right," Lane replied apologetically, "Anything electronic is subject to electronic control."

Rob nodded with a rueful smile.

"What do you make of Doyle's threat?" Lane asked. Lane had already told Rob of Doyle's visit, including what Doyle had said about watching his step in the dangerous sport.

"Presents a serious escalation," Rob replied. He added, "I'm consulting with my security team. We're still on for Darlington. Given Doyle's threat, I just wish our plans were ready for next week at Kansas instead. Can you hold on for one more week?"

Lane nodded, saying, "Wrecks happen just about every which way as it is. How much worse could it be if the council were behind a wreck?"

Rob gave Lane a sidelong glance as they approached the airport drive. Lane was already sorry he'd said what he'd said. A planned wreck could indeed be a whole lot worse.

"We'll take a close look at it," Rob said again, adding, "But we're almost there. Just Kansas to go, and then we'll be on go for Darlington."

Lane nodded again.

Lane didn't sleep well that night, even though the relatively short flight back to Charlotte got Lane back to his condominium at a reasonable hour. The little sleep that Lane did get filled with dreams and nightmares.

Up very early in the morning, Lane decided to head to the race facility to get an early start to the day. When he arrived before seven, though, the lights were already on in the office suite. Someone had also already made coffee in the commissary. As Lane poured himself a cup, he heard someone enter the room behind him. Turning, he saw the team owner.

"Oh, hey," the team owner said, "I was just coming back for a cup. Looks like it's ready."

Lane nodded with a smile.

"You're in awfully early," the owner said to Lane with a return smile.

"I'm early?" Lane said with another smile, adding, "What time did you get in?"

The owner chuckled, answering, "My usual 6:30."

"What time would you come in if I got here tomorrow at 6:30?" Lane asked, teasing the owner with his own chuckle.

"Probably around 6:15," the owner quipped back. They both chuckled.

"Sounds like you're more than just an early riser," Lane observed.

"I've always felt I should lead by example," the owner said with a note of reflective seriousness. He added, "We ask everyone to work hard here at the shop. I don't figure it's fair that I put in fewer hours than the rest of you."

Lane nodded appreciatively.

"Besides," the owner added, "These early hours in the morning are when I'm most able to think uninterrupted about what's most important."

Lane nodded again. He knew what the team owner meant. Lane, like his dad Blake, was a thinker. He didn't feel right about action until he had thought its fit and consequences through. Lane didn't mind making mistakes. He could learn from his mistakes just as much as anyone. Lane just didn't want to make mistakes for lack of consideration.

Some people think the world has too much thinking in it. Lane generally felt the opposite, that the world has far too little thinking in it.

"Looks like you just might make it to Darlington after all," the owner observed.

Lane shook his head, wearing a pained smile and saying, "Looks like it's going to be touch and go. But we'll make it, one way or the other."

"Remember," the owner said with a kind smile, "I'm with you. Every step of the way."

Lane nodded, dropping his head and turning so that the owner couldn't see the tears forming in his eyes. Lane raised his cup of coffee toward the owner in silent salute and slipped out, back to his office, where he sat behind his desk and sobbed. Weeks of pent-up emotion poured out.

Soon, Lane rose from behind his desk to walk through the still-quiet facility. His walk took him to the assembly room, where just a week before they had danced away Darnell's win.

Suddenly, Lane had the strongest desire to see Elena. He didn't even know why. But he headed back to his office, grabbed his bag and keys, and headed out. Texting Elena, he said he'd pick her up in a few minutes.

Elena was outside Rob and Marla's house, waiting for Lane, when Lane pulled up. Elena hopped in beside Lane, and they were off, to nowhere in particular.

As soon as Elena got in his car, Lane found that he had something he wanted to tell Elena. He hadn't thought he'd have anything special to say. He had instead expected that they'd make small talk, take a drive, and just enjoy one another's company for a bit of the morning.

But instead, Lane found himself telling Elena that he didn't know what was going to happen at Kansas that coming weekend, except that it wouldn't be good. And he wanted Elena to know that whatever happened to him, he loved her. Lane told Elena that whatever happened at Kansas, he would be with Elena forever.

Elena listened to every word Lane said with perfect attention, greatest expectation, and deepest embrace. Elena hadn't told Lane, but just before Lane had texted her early that morning, she had an equally compelling desire to reach Lane. His text had come at the perfect moment. And his words as they drove had come with the perfect message, one that her heart fully received.

When Lane had finished, Elena placed her hand gently on his shoulder, then rubbed the back of his neck, then stroked his hair. They drove quietly through the beautiful rolling countryside, until the spell had broken. Elena offered to drop Lane off at the race facility to pick him up with his car again at the end of the day. They hadn't said much of anything else, but their hearts had spoken volumes to one another.

Lane carried the thought through the rest of his work day. He and Elena would be together for the rest of their lives. Elena carried the same thought through her day. Neither was ready to speak with the other about it. Only their hearts, not their minds and mouths, had settled on it. And they both knew Lane had a great challenge to overcome before they might speak of it. One best not start a new life with old burdens.

Lane also had the sense that the coming race at Kansas Speedway was one of the last boxes to check before that old burden lifted. He didn't share his sense with the crew chief and race engineer that survival was his Kansas strategy, as they studied car setups and race strategy throughout the day. But survival was Lane's primary Kansas objective. He wanted to live to race at Darlington, where he expected Rob's plan to carry the day.

Throughout the day, the crew chief proposed several bold measures to, as the crew chief put it, get Lane *over the finish line*. The crew chief's sense was that the race team was so close to winning that one or two more bold adjustments would make up the small difference.

The crew chief's ideas included car balance changes, off-schedule pit strategies, and even changes to the pit crew's roles. The ideas were creative. They were also sound. They were even enticing. But Lane rejected every one of them, one by one, throughout their long race-preparation meetings.

Lane didn't want to change anything. Lane's view was that the team's cars were performing well enough and that they only needed to consistently reproduce their performances over time, for wins to follow. Lane wanted to make only incremental changes, the kind of small tweaks that winning race teams make to stay ahead of the competition.

In Lane's view, the team had already caught the competition. The team just needed to keep competing at a high level. Bold adjustments could throw off the team, sending the car backward and requiring more bold adjustments to catch up, in a never-ending spiral from failure to failure.

In the end, Lane's stance won out. The crew chief conceded. The crew chief and race engineer would help the mechanics make a few small adjustments to the car, advancing things Dover and the prior races had taught them. But they would take no big swings with car setup and no bold risks with race strategy.

It had been a difficult day, and both Lane and the crew chief felt that the difficulties between them weren't necessarily over. For Lane, the lingering disagreement with his crew chief added another cloud, along with Doyle's threat, to the Kansas race. Elena and

Dani were not traveling to the race, leaving another hole in Lane's race weekend.

Lane nonetheless looked forward to being at the race track itself.

Kansas Speedway, among the newer stock-car tracks, has a traditional tri-oval design. The front straightaway of its mile-and-a-half layout bulges out toward the grandstand. The bulge requires a subtle and exciting turn directly in front of the grandstand. The bulge also allows for a long and straight pit road in front of the grandstand, for favorable spectator views of pit road adventures.

Progressive banking up to twenty degrees around the two big oval curves allow for multiple racing lines, once the track rubbers up and comes in. Lights for night racing in the Spring, club suites at two turns, a large spectator viewing area for the race garages, and a casino right alongside the track, add to the track's allures, making Kansas a popular Midwest venue for drivers, crews, and fans alike.

Lane's car unloaded fast. Lane put up some of the fastest practice times, although as good as the times were, he ran only a few practice laps.

Darnell had a fast car, too. Darnell enticed Lane into a friendly wager: whoever qualified fastest would get to choose the place where the loser must buy the winner dinner.

Unfortunately for Darnell, Lane won their qualifying competition easily. Lane qualified in the top five, while Darnell qualified well back in the pack. Lane threatened to choose a famous Kansas City steakhouse for his victory dinner, but circumstances frustrated the outing.

They feasted at a local fast food outlet instead, where Lane paid for their meals anyway, to Darnell's amusement.

The friendship of Lane and Darnell had grown strong and close over the first half of the regular season of racing. That growth was a good thing. Rob's plan to foil the council would soon test their bond.

For Lane, race day seemed to last way too long. His excitement and trepidation over the race had him awake in the motorhome early, even though he had planned to sleep in. With the race at night, he had a long day ahead of him.

To fill the time, Lane went for an early morning walk around the track grounds. He ate breakfast with his pit crew. He hung around the race garage, chatting with Darnell, the crew chief, the race engineer, the mechanics, and anyone else who seemed to have something interesting or valuable to say.

Lane also spent time greeting race fans at the edge of the garage viewing area. Lane was growing more comfortable in his interactions with race fans. He had learned to parry their awkwardness and nervousness around racing stars, not that he considered himself or any of his fellow drivers a star.

Fans, though, do. Fans elevate race drivers. That elevation had initially amused Lane. He had, for a while, tried to diminish it. But amusement and diminishment isn't what fans expect when revealing their admiration for a race driver's skill and accomplishments. Amusement can seem like disrespect for the fan and for the sport.

Lane soon learned to embrace the fans' admiration, not as if it were for him personally but instead as devoted to the sport itself. Lane surely felt that Cup racing deserved admiration. Cup racing is in itself an extraordinary achievement, not just in the technical design of the cars and track but in the spirit of the whole invention.

When Lane arrived at a track, fresh from a week of race preparation, the tracks, cars, haulers, grandstands, and their whole affair still made him feel a degree of awe. He never wanted to lose that feeling. He even suspected that he'd retire and find something better to do, when a race weekend no longer struck a note of wonder within him.

Whenever Lane engaged race fans at a track, he tried to think of their own sense of wonder at the spectacle of it all. He tried to think of how that wonder, communicated to the drivers in heart-felt words of appreciation and respect, lifted them in their own lives. Lane wanted his interactions with fans to increase, not diminish, their reverence for the sport, out of which they just might be drawing a broader reverence for life.

The day eventually wore on to pre-race festivities, including driver introductions and, finally, the prayer and anthem. It was finally time for Lane to get in his car and get on with the race, whatever the race would bring.

The early part of the race reminded Lane of why he loved racing. As is often the case, the drivers spent the first few laps sorting out their cars and track position, getting a feel for the track surface and the relative speed and handling of their car around their competition.

Lane loved that aspect of racing, as the mind and body absorb, process, analyze, and respond to a race's extraordinary sensations. Lane once realized that race driving is a bit like taking control of the tiny car on a wild roller coaster. The roller-coaster ride itself is extraordinary enough, taking every bit of concentration just to endure the ride's wild sensations. Imagine trying to steer the roller-coaster car around its crazy course.

Lane easily held his own near the front of the pack. He could tell that his car, now in race trim, had retained its practice and qualifying speed. His car was also handling well, better than some of the cars around him. Lane soon navigated his way forward into third place and then second place.

As Lane followed the leader around the tri-oval layout, lap after lap, he decided that he wasn't going to press for the lead. Race driving isn't always a matter of getting everything out of the car that the car has to give. Indeed, race driving is far more tactical. Drivers wisely save tires, brakes, body panels, splitters, and other equipment and gear for the long run and for the critical parts of a race.

It also just felt incredibly good for Lane to run lap after lap in second place, comfortably ahead of the field, without significant challenge from the rear. Lane could save his car and its equipment, while just enjoying the steady challenge of navigating a traditional tri-oval track.

As the first stage's end neared, Lane listened especially carefully for how his car would respond, lest he face the challenge Dover had brought, affecting his engine control module. But no, Lane felt nothing unusual. The stage ended with Lane holding second place.

The second stage proceeded in similar fashion. Lane held eighth place on the second stage's restart. Most of the field had pitted at the stage break, all but a handful of trailing cars whose drivers had pitted before the stage's end. Those cars now held the lead.

Lane soon picked off those cars one by one, again without pressing the issue or burning up his equipment. Lane knew how to race with a superior car: save the equipment, take what the race gives you, and keep the car in top shape for the sprint to the end.

Lane thus finished the second stage pretty much as he had finished the first stage, in third place, right behind the leaders, and without having used up his car. Lane was finally racing as he had expected all season to race, driving a leading team's superior car, and earning stage points while ready to compete for the win.

Lane began the third stage much like he had begun the second stage, having fallen back to tenth place, behind cars that had pitted before the stage end and thus remained on the track when the rest of the field pitted for the stage break.

The final stage unfolded much like the two prior stages. Lane's superior car began picking off slower cars, cars that their drivers had exhausted to get where they had gotten among the leaders, one by one. As the race's end neared, Lane was in third place and then second place.

This time, though, Lane wasn't going to ride idly along behind the leader. Lane sensed that he had not yet exhausted his car's capabilities. He hadn't yet pressed the issue, to gain the track position he had gained.

So Lane gradually began driving his car harder and deeper into the turns. He began feathering the gas pedal in, earlier and earlier, at corner exit. And he began hunting the leader, letting the leader know that he was pressing for an opening and that the leader had better be prepared to give way.

That opening came with just five laps to go. Driving hard into corner entry, Lane pulled down below the leader, to the inside of the track. Lane's charge was sufficient for his car to clear the leader through the middle of the turn, so that as Lane returned to the accelerator, he could pull all the way up the track in front of the leader, with good momentum for a run down the straightaway.

Lane was in the lead and pulling away for the win.

Lane didn't drive quite so hard into the next turn or the turn after. Nor did he get back to the gas pedal so early on corner exit. He didn't need to do so. He was clear of the next car and not under attack.

Yet as Lane braked into the next corner entry, preparing in another moment to feather in the gas, his engine roared to full throttle, even though he hadn't yet pressed the gas pedal. For the briefest instant, Lane thought of the engine control module. His worst fear of council interference had come true. The car leapt forward into the curve, lost grip, and shot up the track.

Crashes into the wall on corner exit, when a car suddenly loses grip in the middle of the turn, can be among the hardest in the sport. The centrifugal force of the curve launches the car into the wall at an angle that approaches head on. Adding full throttle to the mix vastly increases those forces.

Lane suffered a horrific crash, crumpling the car against the wall and leaving it sliding down the track into the field's path, where it took additional hits from other cars. Doyle's threat had come true.

14

"Talk to us here," the crew chief radioed Lane inside the crumpled car.

A long silence followed.

Soon, though, Billy radioed from atop the grandstand, saying, "We've got movement inside the car."

A moment later, Billy added, "Window nets coming down."

Lane dropping his car's window net let track emergency crews know that he was conscious and prepared to climb out of the remains of the car.

Crews were at the scene within moments. They helped ease a woozy Lane from his car seat, onto the window ledge, and then out of the car. Lane sat down on the track, his back against the crumpled car.

Soon, Lane rose with the help of the emergency crew. He made his way unsteadily to the nearby ambulance for a ride to the infield care center.

The crew cleared the track of wrecked cars and debris, while race officials held the remaining cars on the backstretch under red flag. The race soon resumed, concluding with a thrilling competition to the finish. One of Lane's veteran teammates won the race, auguring a celebration back at the race facility the next day.

In another one of those increasingly common miracles of automotive safety technology, Lane suffered no serious injury. Nor did any other driver involved in the wreck. Lane would be sore for the rest of the week and bruised here and there. Medical personnel later confirmed Lane fit to race the following weekend at Darlington, if Lane felt up to it, which he surely would.

With the race already over by the time Lane was out of the infield care center, he had little to do but to make his way gingerly back to the race garage for a brief visit, before heading to the motorhome to prepare for the flight home late that night.

Lane greeted the crew chief and race engineer at the garage, where the track crew had towed the remains of Lane's car.

"What did the telemetry show?" Lane asked.

"Full throttle in the middle of the turn," the crew chief replied, shaking his head.

"I hadn't even begun to press the gas pedal," Lane said, adding, "The thing just took off."

"That's what it looked like," the crew chief replied, adding, "And that's what telemetry confirms."

"So what's up?" Lane asked.

"Presumably the same engine control module issue," the crew chief replied.

"Well," Lane corrected the crew chief, "You mean the opposite control issue. The last time we had no engine response when we asked for it. This time we had full throttle without asking for it."

The crew chief shrugged. Shaking his head, he replied, "We'll sure be checking it out. We're securing the parts right now."

Billy the spotter had joined them from the back of the race garage. Laying a hand on Lane's shoulder, Billy added, "That was a wild ride, friend. We were worried about you."

"Thanks," Lane replied. Looking down and shaking his head, he added, "I'm sure not ready for that to happen again."

"Want me to walk you to the motorhome?" Billy offered.

Lane shook his head. Giving Billy a weak smile and nod of thanks, Lane turned and ambled slowly and sorely out of the garage. But he paused outside the garage to turn back and call to the crew chief with a brighter smile, "Hey, can you give me that very same car for Darlington? That car was a rocket ship."

The crew chief smiled and nodded.

Lane kept an eye out for the white sedan as he approached the motorhome. It was nowhere in sight. Instead, Rob stood vigil beside his rental car, waiting to help Lane to the airport.

"Let me guess," Rob greeted Lane, "The engine control module again."

Lane nodded with a painful smile.

"Well," Rob said, "That's not going to be a problem at Darlington."

Lane smiled a brighter smile, replying, "No, it's not. And about time we took matters into our own hands."

Rob smiled back, nodding his glad agreement.

Lane didn't make it to the race facility early the next morning. With such a late flight home from Kansas after the night race, Lane wouldn't have been up and at the race facility early in any case. But as sore as he was from the wreck, when he finally got to bed well after midnight, Lane wondered whether he would make it to the race facility at all.

Lane did make it the next day but not until late morning. Elena picked Lane up at his condominium. She was determined to help him through the day and week. They had texted back and forth late the evening before and in the morning, from which Elena had learned that Lane was alright but banged up.

Yet when Lane opened the condominium door, ready to amble painfully out to Elena's car for a ride to the race facility, Elena almost gasped at Lane's condition. Lane moved with an old man's stoop, one step at a time.

Lane noticed Elena's reaction, saying, "I'll be alright. Just give me a few days."

Elena almost cried in sympathy but held back her tears, not wanting to alarm Lane.

"You want to get checked out again?" Elena asked as Lane settled slowly into her car.

"Already scheduled for a follow-up exam this afternoon," Lane replied with a weak smile.

"You sure you're up to going in?" Elena asked.

Lane shook his head with the same weak smile, saying, "No, but no use moping around at home. I'll just take it easy."

Elena nodded. They drove through a fast-food outlet for breakfast on the way to the race facility. At the facility, Elena got out to help Lane to the door, giving him a kiss on the cheek as they parted. Lane moved slowly, gingerly, and painfully through the rest of the day.

To the limited extent that he was up to anything, Lane's complete focus was on ensuring that the crew chief and race engineer prepared the new car for Darlington, just as they had prepared the old car for Kansas.

Darlington presents every driver and crew chief with a unique setup issue. Darlington may be the hardest track for which a race team prepares. One of its nicknames is, after all, *The Track too Tough to Tame*.

The speed of Lane's car at Kansas should have resolved in Lane's favor the lingering tension between Lane and his crew chief over the Kansas car setup. But Darlington was bound to resurrect and exacerbate that driver/crew chief tension.

Darlington's setup difficulty lies in its asymmetrical design, owing to a historical anomaly. One end of Darlington's 1.366-mile oval has a tighter turn than the other end, owing to a minnow pond outside the track, that the track's founder agreed not to disturb. Pinching one end of the track into a smaller, tighter curve means that the two straightaways are not parallel. One end thus turns more, in a larger, longer curve, than the other end.

Darlington, in other words, is two like tracks in one. Each end of its oval requires a different approach, different car setup, and different race tactics.

Those differences are what make for driver/crew chief tensions. Drivers may want the car setup to run one end of the track, the end they generally find more difficult, than the other end of the track. Crew chiefs, though, may have the opposite opinion that the car needs to handle better on the other end due to different tire wear, braking, or other race hazards. Or driver or crew chief may prefer a balance of the two setups, making both ends of the track equally difficult.

Throughout his Monday meetings with the crew chief and race engineer, Lane kept repeating that he wanted the new car's setup to be like Kansas, with no big adjustments. Lane wanted to retain and even build on his Kansas success. The crew chief, though, held to the position that no track is like Darlington and that Darlington required its own setup.

The race engineer tried without success to play referee between Lane and his crew chief. By the end of the day, they were no nearer to agreeing on a setup. They left the question open for the next day, during which Lane would have some simulator time to help the race engineer analyze options.

Rob, not Elena, picked Lane up at the race facility's door at the end of the day. Lane had looked forward to seeing Elena again. But Lane was just as glad to see Rob. He and Rob had important business to address, which was why Rob arranged with Elena to handle Lane's pickup duties.

"Can we talk?" Rob asked Lane as Lane climbed slowly into the car.

"I'm all ears," Lane grimaced as he settled into the passenger seat and strained to get his seatbelt on.

"Did you check out alright?" Rob asked out of concern.

"Doctors said activity as tolerated," Lane winced, adding, "But right now, I'm not tolerating much."

Lane took a deep breath. Noticing Rob's deepening look of concern, Lane added, "The simulator tomorrow will tell a lot about how this recovery is going to go."

Rob nodded. After giving Lane a minute to settle in for the drive home, Rob began.

"Plans are in place," Rob said, explaining, "The team has silent modules ready to launch the moment the race begins. Your car will read like Darnell's car, and his car like yours. Any electronic interference the council attempts won't interfere with you."

Lane nodded, saying with a clear note of regret, "Just Darnell."

"Well, right," Rob said, continuing, "But that's the test authorities demand before taking action."

Lane knew that Rob had been working with federal and state law enforcement authorities for weeks. While law enforcement has extensive expertise in various cybercrimes, especially identity theft, national security hacking, and child pornography, interfering with business and racing operations isn't one of those areas.

Until the criminal allegations reached the level of bribery, match fixing, extortion, and even, with the Kansas wreck, attempted homicide, detectives had been reluctant to get involved in what the parties might have treated and resolved as a civil, contractual matter.

Even when things between the racing community and the council soon took more-serious turns, prosecutors wanted better evidence before pursuing charges. They wanted Rob's security team to show that the council really was able and willing to interfere surreptitiously, electronically, to ensure a race outcome. Prosecutors wanted Rob to show that the council could interfere with another car, not just Lane's car.

That's when Rob's team came up with the idea of swapping the electronic footprint of Lane's car for Darnell's car. They couldn't induce Doyle to affect another driver. His bookmaking client was manipulating the spread on Lane, not Darnell or any other driver. But they might trick Doyle and the council into thinking another driver's car was Lane's car. And if Doyle and the council sabotaged the run of that other car, rather than only Lane's car, they'd have the proof that prosecutors demanded.

"I'm not doing this without us telling Darnell," Lane announced to Rob.

Rob looked from the roadway to Lane and back to the roadway.

"That's not what we planned," Rob replied.

"I might feel differently if it were just ordinary race trickery," Lane explained, adding, "But now that we're facing outright wrecks of the sort I had yesterday, I can't expose anyone to that, unwillingly."

Lane paused before adding, "Especially Darnell."

Rob nodded. After a moment, he took a deep breath and said, "I'll have to talk with my security team."

Lane nodded. After his own pause, he said, "You agree, don't you?"

Rob nodded, saying, "I do. I might have come to that decision even if you hadn't. I'm glad you did so."

They drove on in silence until they reached Lane's condominium.

"Want some dinner?" Rob asked.

"Thanks, no," Lane replied, adding, "Elena's bringing something over in a little bit. I've got to get some rest."

Rob watched Lane get slowly out of the car, with difficulty. Leaning across the passenger seat, Rob called to Lane just before Lane closed the door, "We'll talk with Darnell tomorrow night at our place."

Lane gave Rob a thumbs up and closed the car door.

Elena nursed Lane through the evening, trying to keep him as still and comfortable as possible. She also tried to keep his mood upbeat and light. Elena knew that Lane was fighting a desperate battle. She also knew that he and Rob planned to turn the tide in that battle at Darlington. She just didn't know how.

Lane figured later that Elena's nurturing presence that evening must have had something to do with it. But that night, Lane dreamed vivid dreams that seemed to be pulling the past few months of demonic mysteries together into an other-worldly sense.

Lane's dreams centered on the historic Darlington track. With ground breaking in 1949, Darlington Speedway is among the sport's oldest race tracks. Its founder carved the track out of cotton and peanut fields for the association's stock-car racing, after seeing the huge crowds the Indianapolis Motor Speedway attracted for open-wheel racers.

Darlington is also the perennial host of one of the sport's Crown Jewel races, the Southern 500. Darlington is thus steeped in stock-car history.

A journalist for the sport's early years, Benny Phillips, captured Darlington's peculiar and central place in the stock-car association Cup racing, when he coined another of its nicknames, *The Lady in Black*. Phillips wrote of how the track captured all of the sport's allure while simultaneously reflecting all of the sport's challenges, so that the track was always on a driver's mind. He compared the track at once to both a gorgeous Hollywood actress and a notorious female foreign war spy.

In the early years, the track's owner also recovered the track's asphalt surface with tar sealant, right before each major race. Hence, *The Lady in Black*.

Lane's dreams that night were exactly in that vein. Darlington was at once bringing together all of his dreams, not only for a challenging race win but also for a life with a beautiful woman Elena, and his worst fears, of harm to himself or Darnell in chasing those dreams.

Lane's dreams involved nightmarish encounters with dark, ancient, peculiar, and random consuming demons, out of which Lane struggled to draw a shining dawn through which he could just see, if not quite reach, a celebrant Dani and Darnell, and a sparkling Elena.

Lane's dreams confirmed for him in the strangest of ways that his heroic adventure through this Darlington race week would be to draw restoration and new life out of the darkest and most chaotic potential. Darlington was proving to be everything for which stock-car racing imagined it. Darlington's darkness would come before Darlington's dawn.

Lane didn't wake up the next day refreshed. He was still too sore, if anything more so than the prior day. And his dreams had if anything exhausted him further. But Lane did awake with a clarity that he hadn't until then grasped. Lane awoke ready to draw treasures from the mouth of his biggest demons.

Elena was at Lane's door with a ride to the race facility first thing that morning. She winced again when she saw Lane open the door and shuffle to her car. But Elena sensed a new resolve in Lane's demeanor. He looked just a little less sorry for himself and just a little more like her young tiger.

Elena looked over and smiled at Lane beside her in the passenger seat, once he had folded himself painfully in. Lane looked back at Elena with his own smile.

"That's more like it," she said to him, adding, "Good to have you back."

Lane's smile broadened. He asked Elena, "You're coming to Darlington, right?"

She nodded, saying, "Of course. Wouldn't miss it for the world."

"Watching the race from atop the pit box, right?" Lane asked.

"If that's an invitation, I'm accepting," Elena replied with a smile.

"What color are you going to wear?" Lane asked.

Elena laughed, already knowing where Lane was going with his question. She replied, "Why, black, of course. I'm your *Lady in Black*."

They laughed together.

15

"I'm sorry guys," Lane said to his crew chief and race engineer, "But I'm just not up to it yet."

Lane had climbed gingerly into the simulator a few minutes before, wondering if his sore body would let him turn the steering wheel and work the brake and gas pedals. It wouldn't. Every sudden movement brought such aches and pains that Lane began to sweat profusely with the effort. And he couldn't concentrate.

The crew chief and race engineer looked at one another and shrugged. With Lane's lack of concentration and effective effort, they weren't getting any good data anyway.

"This afternoon?" the crew chief asked.

"I doubt it," Lane replied.

"Tomorrow?" the crew chief tried again.

"Maybe," Lane replied with an apologetic smile.

"So you're saying we might not get any good data for analysis at all this week?" the race engineer asked.

"Doing the best I can," Lane replied. He added, "We've already scheduled physiotherapy starting at noon today. They wanted some of the swelling to go down first."

Race drivers suffer a wide range of injuries. Accident injuries can include not just limb fractures but severe harness and other bruising from the sudden deceleration and acceleration events of crashes. The worst bruising, with large hematomas, may require a long period of immobility while the body slowly absorbs the clotted blood. Movement could cause clots to migrate, causing blockages to the heart, brain, or other critical organs, resulting in heart attack, stroke, tissue demise, and even death.

Fortunately, Lane hadn't suffered any fractures. And his bruising wasn't so severe. Doctors hadn't restricted his movement to avoid clotting issues. But Lane had the severe joint, bone, muscle, and other tissue pain characteristic of high-speed accidents.

Race drivers soon learn from their crashes that time is generally the only effective remedy to get over the soreness. Physiotherapy, in the form of massage, stretching, electrical stimulation, ice baths or other cryotherapy, and mild exercise or movement, may help. With the special rigors of the Darlington race coming up fast, Lane was ready to try anything.

The one thing race drivers generally can't do is medicate away the pain, at least not if they intend to race. Analgesics affect how the brain processes pain. But to race safely and effectively, race drivers need every bit of processing available, especially the processing of physical sensations. You don't want a race driver driving on painkillers. Their driving is already hazardous enough.

In short, Lane was going to have to get over his pain or gut it out during the race. He had no other option.

Lane, the crew chief, and race engineer headed to the crew chief's office. Lane lagged painfully behind. The crew chief and race engineer shook their heads in frustration and disappointment as they settled in at the office. Lane finally caught up and joined them a few moments later. He eased himself into a seat, trying his best to suppress a groan.

"Probably better arrange and prepare a backup driver now," the crew chief observed out loud to no one in particular.

"No way," Lane replied, although he winced from pain as he did so.

"It's just precautionary," the crew chief replied, adding, "Any backup driver is going to need some time to prepare. We can't wait until the last minute."

Lane just shook his head, firmly. The race engineer thought briefly of saying something to mediate the disagreement but then thought better of it.

"So what are we going to do for car setup?" the race engineer asked instead.

"Give me the Kansas car," Lane said, repeating his request of the day before.

"We can't do that," the crew chief replied, adding, "We have to account one way or another for Darlington's distinct turns. I think the setup has to favor the tighter turns. We've got good data from the last Darlington race, where we ran well. Let's go with that and adjust on the fly as needed."

Lane shook his head, replying, "That data wasn't me driving the car. It was my dad. We have different driving styles. And I'd want a balanced car anyway. I'm not going to wall ride around the bigger turns with a setup for the smaller turns."

Both Lane and the crew chief looked at the race engineer for comment. The race engineer just shrugged, having no idea how to move forward. They sat in silence for a few moments before the race engineer spoke.

"We need some direction today, at least to start," he said, adding, "We can't do everything at the last minute. The guys in the shop have got to get on it."

"Let's go talk to the big guy," the crew chief finally said, referring to the team owner.

Lane closed his eyes and quietly shook his head. The last thing he wanted to do was bring a team dispute to the owner. He almost said something sharp to the crew chief. But they had disagreed before the Kansas race, too, when Lane had his way. He didn't want to continue to sow seeds of dissension. He was too sore to put up a good fight, anyway. And he had the whole issue of the council on his mind, too.

The crew chief had already stood up for the walk to the owner's office. The race engineer stood with him. Lane rose slowly from his chair and followed them out.

The crew chief and race engineer were already in the team owner's office when Lane entered the suite. The owner's administrative assistant greeted Lane with a concerned smile.

"Moving kind of slow there, friend," the assistant observed in a kind manner.

Lane returned a weak smile.

"They're waiting for you," the assistant said. She gave Lane a light pat on the shoulder as she walked him to the office door.

The crew chief was already filling the owner in, when Lane entered the office to take the empty seat between the crew chief and race engineer.

The owner smiled at Lane from across the big desk. Interrupting the crew chief, the owner asked Lane, "How are you feeling, kid?"

Lane gave the owner the same weak smile he had just shared with the administrative assistant. But he said, "I'll be alright by Sunday."

The owner nodded. He turned back to the crew chief who resumed the arguments on both the car setup and the need to arrange for a backup driver.

When the crew chief was done, he turned to Lane, waiting for Lane's response. Lane took a deep breath, ready to begin. But the owner held up a hand to stop him.

"Here's what we're going to do," the owner said. "As far as the public is concerned, we're not preparing a backup driver. The kid's said he'll be good to go by Sunday, and we're trusting him. We don't need to fuel a media fire."

The owner paused, taking care to phrase his next words properly. He continued, "I know a certain recently retired driver who would step in for his son if we asked him."

Lane, the crew chief, and the race engineer all raised their eyebrows in surprise. Looking at the crew chief, the owner continued.

"You've got all the car setup numbers and everything else for that backup driver, if we asked him, which we haven't yet done. And no one breathes a word of this suggestion to anyone."

The owner paused to smile, ensuring that they understood that the owner didn't expect any disclosures.

"And set up the car as the kid has asked," the owner concluded with another glance at the crew chief and race engineer, adding with a kind smile toward Lane, "He took a big hit for the team last weekend. I think he's earned our respect."

The owner nodded, signaling that they were to go. As the crew chief and race engineer rose, though, the owner said quietly, "The kid and I have a couple of business matters to discuss. He'll catch up with you."

Lane eased himself back down into the seat from which he had started to rise. When the others had walked out, closing the door behind them, the owner began.

"I've heard Rob's plan," the owner addressed Lane, adding, "And I approve."

The owner paused before adding, "Assuming Darnell agrees, of course. I understand you're speaking with him tonight."

Lane nodded. He felt embarrassed and ashamed that he hadn't brought the question to the team owner yet. For a moment, Lane thought of making an excuse, such as that of course they would have asked the owner for approval. But Lane wasn't sure that was true.

Lane then thought of apologizing. But he also wasn't sure it had been his responsibility to bring the question to the owner. After all, Rob had apparently done so. Lane decided for the moment that he should just accept the owner's admonishment. Lane looked contritely down at his hands, hoping the owner would continue. He soon did.

"You'll recall that sponsors were going to reassess after Darlington," the owner resumed. When Lane nodded, the owner continued, "That's still their plan. We've got a meeting with them on Monday."

Lane wanted to show his concern rather than just sit silently. And he was frankly curious how sponsors would take his strong racing but generally poor race results, other than at Tallahassee.

"How's that looking?" Lane asked.

"Hard to tell," the owner replied, adding, "Your screen-time numbers have been pretty strong."

The owner was referring to the seconds that Lane's car, festooned with sponsor paint schemes and logos, appeared on television broadcasts and other publicly consumed race video. Race video, engaging fans in the sport, has a higher advertising value than commercials run during breaks from the competition.

The owner shook his head with a rueful smile, saying, "A late-race wreck while in the lead, like you had at Kansas, can be nearly as good as a race win. But sponsors at our level pay for wins."

The owner paused. He looked briefly at Lane to assess what Lane would most benefit from hearing. The owner saw a young racer from royal racing lineage, ready to add to his lineage's luster with his own rare talent and deep devotion. The owner also saw a young racer nearly broken by the sport's extraordinary demands.

"You've been racing heroically with a severe handicap about which sponsors and fans likely won't ever know," the owner said sympathetically.

The owner paused again. Stealing another glance at Lane, the owner decided his young racer, though nearly broken, still needed to hear what every racer needs to know.

"I can't blame sponsors if they pull back for lack of wins," the owner continued, adding, "We'll make the necessary adjustments, more likely to peripheral staff than to things a driver would notice."

Lane knew that the owner was trying to put the sponsor issues in the best light. But the owner's words somehow hit Lane harder than if the owner had said that Lane's own job was on the line.

Still sitting across from the owner, Lane thought of the *peripheral staff* to which the owner had likely referred. They were doubtless the newer mechanics and younger office staff who worked for Lane's race team so valiantly and with such excitement and joy. They all had hopes, dreams, and ambitions. Many of them also had family members dependent on their income.

For a moment, Lane felt the full weight of responsibility for those precious souls.

But quickly, Lane's burden turned from self-pity over his own burden to anger toward the council. He would have won at least one race and maybe more, but for the council's interference. He and the owner wouldn't even be having this conversation if it were not for the council.

Lane looked up at the owner with a fierce look of determination, saying, "Thank you. Are we done?"

The owner raised his eyebrows, pleased and surprised at Lane's determined look. He had tested his young driver once again, and once again his young driver had passed.

"Go get 'em, tiger," the owner said with a smile.

Lane rose quickly, despite the pain. And wincing, he hustled out of the owner's office. No more ambling. No more wallowing.

As Lane passed the office of the drivers' scheduling secretary, he poked his head in, saying only, "Cancel my therapy."

The secretary was about to protest but, seeing Lane turn away and storm off, nodded and shrugged, while reaching for the telephone to make the cancellation.

Lane passed his own office, heading straight for his crew chief's office. Poking his head in, Lane instructed the crew chief, "Fire up the simulator."

The crew chief and race engineer looked up at Lane. The crew chief began to protest, "But the data won't be any good with you...." But Lane had already headed off to the simulator room.

Lane pressed painfully on through hours of simulator training. By the end of the day, Lane's crew chief and race engineer had enough simulator data to adjust their Kansas car setup for Darlington.

"This will do it," the crew chief told Lane as the crew chief poked his head into Lane's office, where Lane had dragged himself after the simulator sessions. The crew chief held up a tablet of simulator data. He added, "We've already got the crew working on the car setup."

Lane looked up from his computer screen, where he had been poring over the team's internal notes and data on drivers, cars, and the track. Lane nodded briefly before returning to his studies.

"Thanks," the crew chief interjected, "You gave us just what we needed."

Lane looked up briefly again, saying, "No. Thank you," before again returning to his studies.

The crew chief smiled in appreciation for his driver as he walked away.

Lane welcomed the family time at Rob and Marla's house that evening with Elena, Dani, and Darnell. Lane needed a break. He needed food and refreshment. And he needed Darnell's light and happy spirit, Dani's smile, and Elena's warm and encouraging presence.

As they enjoyed dinner and conversation, Lane tried to push all thoughts out of his mind of the coming race, confrontation with the council, and sponsor meeting following the weekend. Lane couldn't quite manage to banish the thought, though, that he and Rob would meet with Darnell later that evening about Darnell's critical role in confronting the council.

Elena, too, seemed to Lane to carry a weight that evening that she had until then mostly avoided. Elena had managed to watch Lane's struggles from a respectable distance, until Lane's serious accident the prior weekend.

Lane's wreck, and his lasting soreness, had brought home for Elena just how hazardous Lane's situation had been. Elena felt bad that she hadn't been as compassionate toward Lane as she could have been and hadn't made a greater effort to support him.

Elena recalled the tenderness Lane had shown toward Elena in the week leading up to the Kansas race, when Lane must have known of his impending hazard. She tried that evening to show Lane the same tenderness. And to Elena, Lane appeared to be appreciating her attention and tenderness deeply.

The time soon came for Rob, Lane, and Darnell to move to the den, while Marla, Elena, and Dani enjoyed coffee, cookies, and girl talk at the kitchen table. Rob tried not to signal anything too serious to the women, as he, Lane, and Darnell took their leave of the women. But Marla took a deep breath as the men left, one that Elena and Dani picked up and imitated. Everyone knew something big was up.

Darnell was the first to speak, once they had settled into the den.

"So what's the big plan?" Darnell asked lightly, adding, "Everyone seems more than a little uneasy."

Rob looked at Lane who looked back. They both began to speak to Darnell at once. They both stopped.

Lane said to Rob, "You go ahead."

Rob replied, "No, you first."

Lane then explained to Darnell that Rob and his security team had been monitoring the council's interference with Lane's races since early in the year.

"No kidding," Darnell replied matter of factly, adding, "That council has screwed you over royally."

Lane and Rob raised their eyebrows, surprised at Darnell's candor and insight.

"Well," Lane added, "It got worse at Kansas."

"It sure did," Darnell quickly agreed, adding, "They nearly took you out long term."

Once again, Lane and Rob raised their eyebrows at Darnell's knowledge.

Noticing their surprise, Darnell said, "Come on. Everyone knows what's going on."

Lane shook his head, saying, "No, buddy. We think that they're manipulating my engine control module mid race."

Darnell said simply, "Not surprising. They seem to be manipulating a lot of other things."

Seeing the need to cut to the chase, Rob interjected, addressing Darnell by saying, "We've got a big request to make of you."

Darnell looked at Rob with a shrug, inviting Rob's request.

"We want to swap electronic footprints between your car and Lane's car for the Darlington race," Rob said to Darnell.

"Go for it," Darnell replied instantly, with another shrug. He added, "Anything else you need from me?"

Rob shook his head, saying with deep seriousness, "You don't understand. That means that if the council wants to wreck Lane again, it'll instead wreck you."

Darnell shook his head. Looking at Rob with more than a hint of anger, Darnell replied, "No. You don't understand. It's about time your team did something. Bring it on."

Darnell rose, turned, and walked to the door of the den. With his hand on the door handle, he turned back to Rob and Lane saying, "Care for some cookies?"

Rob and Lane looked at one another with a smile, shaking their heads in disbelief.

"Guess not, then," Darnell said with his own smile, adding, "Just means more for me, then."

Darnell opened the door to the den and walked out.

16

"Would you like to take a trip on Monday?" Lane asked Elena as the miles on the way to Darlington ticked by.

Elena looked from the road to Lane in the passenger seat beside her. They'd left Charlotte Thursday mid-morning and would be to Darlington shortly after noon. Elena had offered to drive to spare Lane the effort and discomfort.

"What did you have in mind?" Elena replied.

"Just a day away from everything, just to ourselves," Lane replied.

Elena glanced at Lane again with a smile. Lane smiled back.

"Let's see that you're up to it, first," Elena replied. She gave Lane a brief pat on his leg before returning her free hand to the steering wheel.

Elena's heart wanted to leap at Lane's suggestion. But Elena had decided to practice a little more compassion, at least until Lane had fully healed. Still, though, Elena wondered what plans Lane might have for Monday. She hoped they were good plans, maybe even big plans.

The motorhome was already in place when Lane and Elena arrived. Lane was eager to get to his race garage to see the team's progress. But Elena prevailed on Lane to pace himself, letting the team finish the garage setup while Lane rested in the motorhome.

Dani and Darnell soon joined Lane and Elena in the motorhome. Dani and Darnell had also driven down to Darlington together. They had texted Lane and Elena for fast-food orders, which they brought with them to the motorhome.

As the four of them enjoyed their meal, Dani asked Lane and Elena, "What are you doing Monday? Darnell and I were thinking of an outing."

Elena smiled but looked at Lane. Lane glanced back at Elena before replying to Dani, "We've already got a date planned for the day. Sorry."

Dani stuck her lower lip out in an exaggerated pout. Darnell, Lane, and Elena laughed.

"Let us know if you change your mind," Dani invited Lane with a wink.

Lane smiled and shrugged. Elena wondered again what Lane had in mind for Monday.

Lane and Darnell were soon off to their race garages, once again side by side in the garage complex.

Dani and Elena had promised to help Marla with some of Marla's own setup for the race team she and Lane's dad Blake ran in the level below the Cup series.

Blake, indeed, would be attending his first race of the year. He had deliberately stepped out of the picture after his retirement at the end of the prior season, especially with his son Lane taking his driver's seat. Darlington would be Blake's public return, only in the role of an owner of his second-level team.

Lane spent the afternoon in his race garage watching the crew chief and race engineer go over his car with the help of the race mechanics. The crew chief periodically conferred with Lane, explaining what they were doing, and confirming with Lane that they were making the right adjustments. Darnell did likewise in his neighboring race garage.

Late in the afternoon, Rob stopped by the race garages, inviting Lane and Darnell for a walk. It wasn't a social occasion. Rob wanted to update Lane and Darnell on his team's plans and preparation for the electronic footprint swap. And an open air walk around the grounds seemed the most-secure location for a confidential chat.

The three ended up in the grandstand, leaning on a railing overlooking the track and garages.

"The footprint swap is going to throw your crew chiefs off on race data," Rob warned. He added, "They'll be looking at data from the other car, without knowing it."

"That's okay," Darnell replied with a grin, "We don't listen to them anyway."

Lane chuckled. But he had a thought.

"What about the spotters?" Lane asked. He explained, "If we really needed to get information on our own cars, they might be able to share that information back and forth."

"Too much of a disclosure risk," Rob added, shaking his head. He explained, "We've got to rely on the two of you and no one else."

"Do you think they'll figure it out anyway?" Lane asked, adding, "Billy's got a sixth sense when it comes to spotting issues."

"Maybe," Rob replied, tipping and nodding his head in acknowledgment. Lane's spotter Billy may well figure out the anomaly, Rob knew. But Rob also trusted that Billy would use his information circumspectly. Rob concluded, "It's just a risk we'll have to take."

"So what's the worst that could happen with this swap plan?" Darnell asked, more curious than worried. He was instead relishing the challenge.

"Confusion," Rob answered, explaining, "If each of you can keep your focus on what you are experiencing and observing, you should be alright. But if your crew chiefs, race engineers, or spotters start to confuse things for you, or if you start to rely on the data that we know you can't trust, then we may be in for it."

Lane and Darnell both nodded.

"Are you sure this plan is going to get you the evidence you need?" Lane asked in conclusion.

"Our team has everything monitored," Rob replied, adding, "If the council interferes electronically, we'll have what we need."

Lane and Darnell nodded again. Lane, though, pointed to the race garages, where a white sedan had just pulled up.

"Looks like we better be going," Lane said, adding, "Someone seems ready to pay us a visit."

Darnell was the first to reach his race garage. Lane, still slowed from his soreness, strolled into his adjacent garage shortly later. They had each passed the white sedan outside the race garages. Its tinted windows had prevented them from discerning who occupied it.

They need not have wondered. Lane soon noticed Doyle standing outside the two garages, watching the mechanics work on the cars. Lane caught Darnell's eye in the back of the adjacent garage, tipping his head toward Doyle. Darnell nodded.

Lane didn't want to encounter Doyle. Lane had nothing to say to him, nor nothing he wanted to hear Doyle say. But as Lane patiently waited in the back of his garage for Doyle to leave, he began to think he would have no choice but to encounter him.

Lane was right. Doyle soon stepped into Lane's garage, looking toward Lane for an acknowledgment. Lane breathed a deep sigh. He stood upright from his heavy lean on the counter in the back of the garage, to make his way toward Doyle.

"Ah," Doyle said to Lane with a mock voice and expression of concern, as Lane slowly approached, "You are looking sore. What an awful wreck that was last weekend."

Lane shrugged, without changing his expression or taking his eyes off Doyle. Lane simultaneously suppressed all thoughts of making any retort.

"Have you thought of letting your father drive for you this weekend?" Doyle asked with mock sympathy. He added with a sly smile, "Surely he's well qualified to tame the track that's too tough to tame."

Lane shifted his gaze from Doyle's face to looking over Doyle's shoulder at the bright sky outside. Lane simply wasn't going to honor Doyle with a reply. Someone else was, though.

"So you've seen his dad drive, huh?" Darnell said to Doyle from over his shoulder. As Doyle turned to regard the interloper with a superior look, Darnell added appreciatively, "That man could surely drive a stock car."

"We were just going to have a little chat, if you don't mind," Doyle began to answer Darnell. But Darnell cut Doyle off even before Doyle had finished.

Sticking his greasy hand out in front of him for a handshake, Darnell asked, "What's the name? I don't think I caught it."

Doyle recoiled from Darnell's proffered hand, nearly in horror. But Darnell had stepped and reached so far forward toward Doyle that Doyle couldn't avoid it. Doyle took Darnell's hand with great reluctance.

Darnell gave Doyle's hand a firm shake. Letting go of Doyle's hand, Darnell pulled a red grease rag from his back pocket, wiped his own hand, and offered Doyle the rag, saying with a chuckle, "What's a little grease between friends, eh?"

Mechanics who had already turned to watch the confrontation chuckled along with Darnell. They began to drift forward out of the farthest reaches of the two adjacent garages, anticipating a good show.

"Hey, sorry to interrupt you two," Darnell addressed Doyle but with a glance to Lane. Darnell added to Doyle, while nodding toward Lane, "What's that little chat you wanted to have with my friend."

"I – I...," Doyle stammered, but Darnell cut him off again.

"Hey, you're not an IRS man, are you?" Darnell asked Doyle with a frown, adding, "Or maybe one of those regulators? What do you call it, the ATF or the EPA or some such thing?"

The closing circle of mechanics laughed. Doyle shook his head, saying, "No, no, not the IRS or EPA. Just checking in on your friend."

"Well hey, buddy," Darnell addressed Lane, "He says he's just checking in on you. Do you have anything in mind he can do for you?"

Lane shook his head. Now playing along, Lane deliberately echoed words Lane had said to Doyle many weeks earlier, "I just want to win races."

The mechanics in the circle around them nodded appreciatively. Murmurs of *He just wants to win races* went up, as the mechanics chuckled some more.

"Is that good enough?" Darnell asked Doyle, who looked increasingly uncomfortable, as if he was about to run.

When Doyle didn't immediately respond, Darnell asked him again, "Anything else you want to say to my friend before you get back in that meter reader outside and disappear into the ether?"

The circle of mechanics laughed at Darnell's description of the white sedan. Appreciative murmurs of *meter reader* and *into the ether* went up, to more chuckling.

Angered, Doyle tried to compose himself, to once again claim the upper hand. He shot back, "Just watch your backs. I hear Darlington is an especially dangerous *lady in black*."

The mechanics all emitted mock sounds of fright, *whooo!*, as laughter erupted. Doyle pushed his way through the scrum toward the open garage door, to calls of *back to the meter reader!* and more laughter.

When Doyle had gone and the circle of mechanics had broken up, Lane smiled broadly at Darnell while shaking his head. Lane quipped, "He's not taking kindly to that. I hope it doesn't cost us in the race."

"Look," Darnell replied, "He doesn't know what he's talking about. If they mash my accelerator like they did yours, I'm just going to ride it all the way around the wall like the famous *Hail Melon*."

Darnell was referring to the world-famous incident in which a Cup playoff driver had floored his accelerator around the last curve of the last lap, violently riding hard up against the wall, passing just enough cars to qualify for the Cup championship. Fans instantly called it the *Hail Melon* after the racer's farm sponsor, the football tactic of a last-gasp fifty-yard pass, and the traditional prayer.

The *Hail Melon* happened at Martinsville Speedway, not Darlington. But as close to the wall as cars ran at Darlington, a *Hail Melon* at Darlington might not be out of the realm of possibility. Yet the strategy had carried such tremendous risk to car, driver, competitors, and fans that the stock-car association had promptly outlawed it.

Lane laughed at the thought. It sounded like just the sort of thing Darnell would do, too, if it were still legal.

"So," Lane said to Darnell, "Practice tomorrow, qualifying on Saturday, and the race on Sunday. How about dinner for four tonight?"

"You're on," Darnell said, adding, "Dani and I will pick you and Elena up at the motorhome in an hour."

Lane thought for a moment before adding, "You know what? Can we make it dinner for six? I'd like to make another invite."

Darnell shrugged, replying, "Sure. Bring your mystery guests." Even as he said so, Darnell had an idea of whom Lane was about to invite.

When Darnell and Dani pulled up outside the motorhome an hour later, Blake and Diana, the parents of Lane and Dani, were standing outside chatting with Lane and Elena.

"Mom! Dad!" Dani greeted them as she jumped from Darnell's car.

Blake and Diana embraced Dani in one big hug. Lane joined them.

Blake's decision to stay away from the race tracks for a while had been a good one. Lane and Dani had filled the space their absence left with good things, including especially their dating relationships and growing friendships and closeness with Elena and Darnell.

But the time seemed right for Blake and Diana to visit the tracks again. Blake had his race team to lead with his sister Marla. Blake wanted to be involved at the tracks, not just back at his race facility, with the team's drivers whom he wished to coach and mentor.

Yet Blake and Diana also wanted to share Lane's professional and personal growth from a respectful, but still close, distance. They also wanted to get to know Darnell and to watch his relationship with both Lane, as a teammate, and Dani, as a boyfriend, grow.

Blake and Diana had enjoyed their months away from the sport, their first time away from the sport during its season in a couple of decades. But they had also missed the community, missed the friendships, and missed the excitement and rhythm of the racing.

The six of them made their happy way to the small city's favorite music and food venue. With the racing community in town, they felt like they knew everyone at the venue.

Blake and Diana spent much of the evening visiting tables and receiving visitors at their table, catching up on family and community news. In the middle of the evening, Diana leaned over to whisper to Blake how much she had missed the camaraderie. Blake agreed. They vowed not to leave their connections so long unattended again, without at least equally good reason.

Lane and Elena felt something special that evening, too. Although Lane's parents were present, Lane and Elena were no longer the kids in the community. Blake's retirement and absence, and Lane's second season of Cup racing, his first for Blake's old team, had given Lane the current standing within the racing community that Blake had once enjoyed. Lane was the racer now, not his dad. And Lane and Elena felt that recognition and respect throughout the large room.

Dani and Darnell also felt something new and special that evening. The presence of Dani's parents Blake and Diana had the not-so-subtle effect of blessing Dani's dating relationship with Darnell. If Darnell had been an add on, afterthought, or adjunct to Dani's royal racing family before that evening, after that evening, he was certainly less so. Depending on how things went between Darnell and Dani in the near future, the evening could as well have been Darnell's public induction into the family.

That is how many sound communities treat their members, as woven into the community through their subset families. Try to enter some communities without a family connection, and it may take years to gain trust and acceptance. Enter a community as a close friend or outright blood member of one of the community's leading families, and you are in, no questions asked.

Blake and Diana, Lane and Elena, and Dani and Darnell didn't yet know that their splendid evening would prove to be just one of several poignant Darlington moments, moments that a skilled photographer might have captured to share a generation, or two or three generations, later. Families have those moments when everyone present knows that time and space have frozen the setting into a cross-generational memory.

The more of those moments a family enjoys, the greater the family's blessing can be, although a single such moment of the right composition, quality, and spirit can suffice eternally.

The evening was over too soon for all six of the celebrants. Yet in its own way, the evening never ended. Love had etched its poignant memory into eternity.

17

"This is going to be wild," Darnell said to Lane at their race garages the next morning, as they prepared for practice.

"What, practice?" Lane asked, adding, "I hope not."

"No," Darnell replied, "Your crazy plan to swap electronic footprints during the race."

Lane shrugged. He'd been having the same thought but explained, "It's supposed to help make the case against the council, I guess."

"No, I'm fine with it," Darnell replied again, adding, "It will be like racing as a kid, with no data but only your dad in your ear."

Lane laughed. He remembered when his dad Blake would spot for him in his go-kart races, cheering him on, encouraging and guiding him around and around the little dirt tracks.

"That's my plan, too," Lane replied to Darnell, explaining, "I'm going to listen to Billy and not much else. It will be like racing should be, driver, machine, and track."

Darnell nodded, saying, "Exactly what I mean."

Practice went well for both Darnell and Lane, proving that they had fast cars with decent setups. Their crew chiefs made only a few adjustments drawn from their practice experience and results.

Practice once meant running lap after lap, interspersed with frantic adjustments to the car to get back on track for more practice. Simulator data and computer analysis of hundreds of potential setup options had reduced practice to a few laps mostly to shake down the cars. Many race weekends skipped practice entirely because of weather, travel schedules, or other causes and conveniences.

Drivers had once also spent days at tracks all over the country, testing cars and equipment. Drivers might test at a track for a full day or two, running lap after lap with various setups, cars, and equipment. Testing might occur weeks or even months ahead of when the drivers would return to the track for a race. Testing, though, like practice, had mostly disappeared, a victim of both economics, because testing was expensive, and of data analysis.

With practice out of the way, Lane and Darnell could look forward to qualifying the next day, around the second-level series race. Cup drivers often try to watch the second-level series race, either in person, on television, or on video delay. Cup cars differ markedly from the somewhat slower and much less expensive cars run in the second-level series. But cars are cars, and watching the second-level cars work lines up and down the track as they raced could teach a Cup driver a thing or two.

Lane had an extra incentive for watching the second-level series race, which was to share it with his dad Blake, whose team had cars and drivers in the race.

They spent the early part of the race in a skybox suite Marla had arranged for sponsors.

Lane was still learning how to communicate with sponsor representatives. Sponsor representatives may have no racing knowledge, coming from the corporate world, or substantial racing knowledge, if the sponsor had hired a motorsports insider to manage the sponsorship relationship. Lane never knew what to assume, often embarrassing himself or the representative with too much or too little insider talk.

Lane watched as Blake interacted with the sponsor representatives. Lane could see that Blake was a master at relationship management. Blake knew most of the representatives, which helped a lot. But Lane saw Blake quickly form relationships with new representatives whom Blake hadn't met before. A personal question or two about kids, racing background, and other interests seemed to do the trick.

But Lane also noticed Blake exercising other skills to build trust and relationships. Lane saw how Blake adjusted his own communication style depending on how the representative he was befriending spoke.

Blake spoke informally with some representatives, like they were old friends or even family members. But Blake spoke professionally with others and in a highly formal manner with a few, each depending on how the representative had spoken. Lane made a note to adopt the communication style of the ones with whom he spoke.

With sponsor representatives befriended, impressed, and at ease, Blake and Lane slipped out of the skybox and down toward the track. Blake started pointing out to Lane things Blake was noticing about the racing lines and tactics, just as Lane did the same to Blake.

Soon, Blake asked Lane point blank, "How are you feeling about tomorrow's race?"

Lane gave his dad a thumbs up. He felt good about his car, a little confused about the electronic-footprint plan, and concerned for Darnell. But Lane didn't feel like talking about it. And Blake understood Lane's preference not to talk.

The time Lane and Blake shared together, leaning on the grandstand railing, watching Blake's team race on the track below, was another one of those poignant moments. It was the first time Lane and Blake had been trackside together, anticipating Lane's Cup race that Blake would watch as a spectator. The generation had shifted, taking its new form.

Fortunately, qualifying went just as well as practice had gone for both Lane and Darnell. The speed their cars had shown in practice carried over to their qualifying runs.

Qualifying results are usually significant, except perhaps at superspeedway tracks where the drivers depend on pack racing. Qualifying well can be especially significant at Darlington because of the track's difficulty in passing. Limited racing lines, narrow straightaways, and constant up-on-the-wheel demands from the distinct turns at the track's opposite ends mean fewer opportunities to pass.

Drivers often just have to let a faster car go by, too, rather than try to defend track position among all the other perils of the track. Starting nearer the front can mean finishing nearer the front. Starting nearer the back can be fatal to the chances of winning or even finishing strong.

Lane, especially, needed to run strong for their plan to work. If, as Doyle had demanded, Lane must not win until later in the season, for Doyle's bookmaking client to reap match-fixing profits, then Lane would need to threaten a win to ensure that Doyle's council interfered. Except that with the swap of electronic footprints, the council's interference would instead affect Darnell, wherever Darnell might be in his position on track.

Lane was among the first cars to qualify, easily posting the fastest time yet. But nearly the whole field was yet to come. One by one, cars ticked off their qualifying times. Most of them were slower than Lane's qualifying time. Only a handful were faster. Lane would start in the fourth row, having qualified eighth. Darnell would start two rows back.

As is common among Cup drivers, Lane and Darnell lingered at their race garages late on Saturday. Doing so can be part of a driver's rhythm in mentally and emotionally preparing for racing.

Cup driving takes extraordinary mental preparation. Unless one is an automaton or psychopath, one cannot generally simply wake up, jump out of bed, and decide to go racing. A driver must prepare the psyche for the shock, risks, and demands of racing.

The sport often sees first-time drivers crash out in the first few laps, even as early as the first lap. Those crashes can be due to the driver's failure or inability to adequately prepare the psyche for racing's full-on assault on the senses.

The first-time driver may have perfectly capable technical driving skills. Simulators and racing experiences in lower levels will have ensured those skills. But the driver must deploy those skills under the enormous weight of a Cup race's full spectacle. And doing so presents a uniquely formidable challenge.

Each driver handles the sheer challenge of starting a Cup race in their own way. Darnell tended to make light humor of the challenges, consistent with his comedic, jokester personality. Lane tended toward the opposite, to immerse himself meditatively in the deep meaning of racing.

That evening, in their adjacent Darlington race garages, Lane and Darnell interacted more than they ordinarily would have. Their growing friendship and increasing time together had begun to knit their different personalities and different racing rhythms together. That interweaving of their souls was, for both of them, a good thing.

Psychologists, cognitivists, and spiritualists suggest that we gain and retain our sanity in communities, rather than alone. The human mind is a wonder. The human brain's prefrontal cortex, integrating consciousness and rationality with the will and emotions, is a spectacular design, arguably the greatest of all designs in the universe.

Yet the prefrontal cortex is also a fatally limited thing. The necessary intensity of its machinations tends to work against itself. Our minds, left alone, dwell obsessively on things best ignored. Bereft of community interactions, we tend to become passive aggressive, compulsive, isolated, delusional, and depressive. Our minds consume ourselves.

Darnell, left alone, might have become a fool, even if an insightful and engaging one. Lane, left alone, might have become a monk, philosopher, or recluse. Darnell and Lane together, informing, buoying, balancing, and levitating one another, proved themselves better individuals and racers.

Blake soon joined them. Having returned to the track from his self-imposed hiatus after retirement, Blake had to find his place. No longer a race driver, Blake had to find those seams and gaps in which the racing community would welcome a retired driver and current team owner.

Blake doubted that a race garage the night before a big Cup race was one of those welcoming places. Blake knew that the race garage the night before a big race is a driver's place for serenity and solitude. But nothing else was going to attract and hold Blake. And Blake felt a special call and affinity for his own son Lane that evening, not that Blake would make such a visit a habit.

Lane and Darnell welcomed Blake's arrival at the race garage. Blake's presence with the two young racers, one his son and the other the boyfriend of his daughter, created yet another one of those poignant moments.

One sees grainy black-and-white photos of a racing patriarch encouraging the patriarch's progeny, when those progeny later went on to their own racing fame and fortune. Those photos tell so much about the racing community, especially its family heritage and values, but also how it values its own history and, even more so, its own future.

No family is sound without both, the ability to look back on itself with gratitude and forward on its future with hope, expectation, and a good degree of confidence. If a photographer had been present at that moment, the shot of Blake chatting amiably with his two young racers, both of whom were looking each day more and more like the sport's future, would have later proven priceless.

Families are wise to collect, share, and celebrate photos like those, evoking such memories and such hope for the future. Organizations, industries, and sports are wise to do the same. We live less on today's meal than on an inheritance from the past and a loan from the future.

With these and other poignant moments, Darlington's lady in black had drawn rare gifts from her ground's darkest corners, with which to encourage and comfort Lane, Darnell, and their teams, friends, and family. Whatever Sunday's Cup race brought, Lane and Darnell could treasure those gifts for a lifetime.

Sunday dawned bright and clear. Yet restless air that augured meteorological and racing uncertainty. It looked like a storm might roll in, both in the atmosphere and among the drivers on the race track.

The order and predictability of pre-race festivities kept the drivers sane and focused. Lane had encouraged Elena to be with him beside his car on pit road for the prayer and anthem. Darnell had done likewise with Dani. Each girlfriend had accepted their driver's invitation. For both dating couples, things felt right, natural, and yet new, fresh, and filled with hope.

With pre-race festivities over, Lane and Darnell each climbed into their cars. As they did so, they each had a moment's thought of the electronic-footprint swap Rob's security team was about to execute. From a virtual perspective, they were right then not climbing into their own car but into the other's car. Each, though, swiftly banished the thought. They had a difficult race to run. A lot depended on the racing and its outcome.

The grand marshal's call came quickly, *Drivers, start your engines!* Engines up and down pit road roared to life.

And at that moment, Rob's security team flipped the switch on the swap of electronic footprints. All telemetry data that Lane's car generated, including acceleration, braking, shifting, steering, engine temperature, track location, track position, speed, distance behind competitors, time behind leader, lap times, and pit road speed, read as if it were Darnell's car, and vice versa.

If the council manipulated Lane's data, it would be manipulating Darnell's car and outcome, not Lane's car or outcome. For the first time all year, Lane would race free of the council's destructive influence. And for the first time all year, Darnell would bear whatever interference, punishment, and penalty the council intended for Lane.

The cars pulled down pit road and onto the track behind the pace car for their warm-up laps. Anticipation for the race's glorious start built across the huge grandstands. Everyone stood as the cars circled the track behind the pace car for the last time. The pace car pulled down onto pit road as the field came around to the starting zone.

And they were off under the green flag.

The shake-down laps early in the race worked to Lane's advantage. With his car having both speed and reasonably good handling at both ends of the track, Lane was able to pick up two spots, as drivers ahead of him, with handling challenges, wisely gave way. Lane moved up from eighth to sixth place.

Darnell also held his own. Starting two rows back of Lane in tenth place, Darnell used the shake down laps to gain a single position into ninth place.

Cars battled respectfully back and forth through the early part of the race, testing their own handling while testing the speed and handling of their competitors. The race soon made apparent which drivers had fast cars, which drivers had the slightly loose cars Darlington seems to prefer, and which drivers had the tight cars that Darlington usually condemns.

Just as teams were beginning to finalize their strategy for the race's first green-flag pit stop, the skies suddenly darkened. The unsettled, warming air had joined with the typically high humidity to congeal a thunderhead over the track. As the first fat drops splattered windshields, race officials called the cars to pit road for a race halt.

Drivers sat slumped in their cars. Fans ran for cover, as the skies unleashed a gully washer. Pit crew hunkered under the pit boxes or ran for the race garages. Nature had come roaring back.

When a natural event interrupts a motorsports race, whether a downpour of rain, a lightning show, or at other tracks a sandstorm, the drivers, crews, and fans often feel frustration, disappointment, and annoyance.

Let the show go on. Leading drivers and their race fans can be especially disappointed when the natural event interrupts a good run that might have soon led to victory.

But sometimes, the natural interruption instead feels heaven sent. Motorsports can be an unrelenting grind, when it comes right down to it. Races one after another can wear down the spirit of some drivers, teams, and race officials. Sometimes, a simple rain interruption can allow drivers to take a refreshing deep breath, right when they would otherwise be up on the wheel, holding onto a desperately fragile car or grinding for track position with a minimally competent setup.

For Lane, Darnell, other drivers, and their teams and race fans, this gully washer had the salutary rather than diminishing effect, especially so because it was so short, so violent, and followed so quickly by spectacular clearing skies.

The brief storm's cleansing of the track would create its own new hazards, requiring drivers to run cautious lap after cautious lap, rebuilding on the track surface the tire rubber that the storm washed away. But the downpour at the same time seemed to wash away the mental and emotional detritus that had accumulated across the length of the half season of racing.

In the instant, racing seemed to have regained its joyful, courageous, confident spirit. The storm had washed away all of the petty machinations of the prior weeks and months, whether by drivers, teams, or the nefarious Doyle and his hated council. Everyone started afresh, including in particular Darnell and Lane.

18

The race soon restarted, after the track crew and bright sunshine dried the surface. All teams used the break in the race for a pit stop, fuel, and four tires. The break had come too close to the first stage's end for any pit strategy. The field would race to the stage's end.

Lane found his car's handling more challenging on the freshly washed track. But so did the other drivers. Everyone hued or tried to hue to a conservative racing line. The few who failed promptly paid for it, with step outs, slides, and, in a few cases, taps of the outside wall. Hardly anyone passed. A few drivers relinquished track position to avert a spinout and potential wreck.

Lane finished the first stage in fifth place. Darnell ran eighth. Both drivers breathed sighs of relief as the field slowed behind the pace car for the stage break.

Drivers, like athletes in other sports, often try to take their competitions in chunks. Athletes find it hard to sustain full effort, attention, and concentration across a long event. So they learn to divide the event up into more-manageable chunks or parts.

In professional basketball and football, those parts are quarters and halves, coming with certainty under game clocks. In baseball, the chunks involve innings, taken one, two, or three at a time until completing all nine.

In Cup racing, the chunks involve the traditional three race stages (four stages at only a single race). When one stage ends, drivers often make a concerted effort to reset and refresh their inner clocks. Crew chiefs and spotters use radio communications to help the drivers with their resets.

"One down, two to go," Lane's crew chief radioed Lane.

Inside the car, Lane raised his helmet visor to rub his eyes. He also settled down in his seat, giving his arms and back a little break from racing up on the wheel throughout the first stage. Any small change in his position could ease the stress, strain, and exhaustion later. As sore as he had been throughout the week, Lane needed the breaks.

The cars soon reassembled in double file for the start of the second stage. And then, they were off under the green flag.

Lane once again held his own on the race's restart. He knew that he would need to continue to do so as the race progressed, and caution flags began to fly. Restarts at any track are important. At Darlington, they can be critical for success.

Lane was glad for the race to unfold through the second stage without multiple restarts or any big wreck. Lane had begun to settle on a strategy of just holding his position until much nearer the end. As long as he was in the top five, Lane felt that he could not press the issue for better track position until perhaps the very last few laps.

Soon, though, Lane heard the radio crackle to life with an unwelcome message.

"We've got a temperature issue," Lane's crew chief radioed Lane. The crew chief added, "What's the gauge say?"

Lane took a quick glance at the gauge, which read fine. He radioed back, "We're alright here," without elaborating.

The exchange was the first clear indication that Rob's plan might well be in place and working, although more time would tell. Lane wondered whether Darnell was in fact having a temperature issue, one that read from the electronic-footprint swap as an issue for Lane.

Lane also wondered whether the council had begun to interfere, seeing that Lane was holding a solid position on track. If so, he hoped that Rob's team was gathering the necessary evidence.

"Better back it down," the crew chief soon radioed Lane, adding, "We're showing the temperature climbing above limits."

Lane ignored the call. His car's temperature gauge showed no such alarm.

"You alright?" Billy the spotter soon radioed Lane, as Lane continued to circle the track without giving any ground to the competition.

"Fine here," Lane radioed confidently back.

Lane guessed that Billy was beginning to detect the anomaly that Rob's plan had introduced into the race. Lane also guessed that Billy would soon be conferring with Darnell's spotter. Lane could see Darnell's car ahead. The leaders had already lapped Darnell, whose car, Lane figured, might have a temperature problem or be suffering other problems or interference.

For the next several laps, indeed for much of the rest of the second stage, Lane parried his crew chief's warnings about engine temperatures, back and forth. Lane's crew chief had expressed greater and greater frustration, as Lane appeared to be ignoring the crew chief's dire warnings, clear instructions, and sound advice.

Lane, though, wasn't at all concerned with his car's condition or performance. His car felt and performed fine, indeed well enough for him to gain two additional track positions. Lane had raced his way into third place.

The crew chief's dispute with Lane over temperature readings came to a head when the field began making green-flag pit stops.

"Coming to you," Lane radioed, indicating to his crew chief that he was preparing to follow the two leaders onto pit road.

"Four tires, fuel, and an engine check," the crew chief radioed back.

"Negative on the engine check," Lane promptly replied, adding, "Just give me the tires and fuel."

"We've got to do something about temperatures," the crew chief replied.

"Car's fine," Lane shot back, adding, "Leave it alone, or I'll just drive off."

The crew chief remained silent on the other end. Billy jumped in with, "All clear for pit road. Bring it on down."

"Fuel and tires only," Lane replied.

"Got it," Billy replied, usurping the crew chief's role.

Billy had understood that Lane needed to know whether the crew chief was going to attempt an engine check. Billy had answered that the crew chief wasn't, even though Billy didn't really know. He had just left the crew chief no choice, clearly overstepping his role in a way that could lose a spotter his job. Lane guessed that Billy had discerned and perhaps even confirmed something that had made it worth that risk.

Lane's pit crew gave him a strong pit stop. As the field emerged, Lane was back on the track right behind the two leaders who had pitted ahead of him. And he held that position for the rest of the stage. Lane finished the second stage in third place.

Darnell, whether due to engine temperature issues or other problems or interference, had struggled. Because he had fallen a lap down, he pitted before the second stage's end and then stayed out when the field came down pit road under the stage end's yellow caution. The strategy gained Darnell little in track position, leaving him near the back of the pack, but put him back on the lead lap.

Elena and Dani had watched the race unfold from atop Lane's pit box. When the downpour came, they huddled with the pit crew beneath the pit box. When the downpour stopped, they helped dry the pit box with towels so that they could return to their seats atop the box.

Dani celebrated with Elena each time Lane finished strong at the end of the first two stages. Elena decried Darnell's issues and losses, right along with Dani. For Dani and Elena, it was a tale of two races, Lane's involving steady success, and Darnell's involving depleting challenges.

Elena and Dani stood atop the pit box, right along with everyone in the huge grandstand, as the field came to the green flag for the final stage's start.

Lane once again held his own on that restart. Lane had chosen to restart in the outside lane behind the leader. The car ahead of Lane in second place had chosen to restart in the inside lane beside the leader. Lane's position immediately behind the leader gave Lane the opportunity to give a helpful shove to the leader, sending the leader back into a clear lead. Lane did as most any trailing driver would have done in his position.

But the final stage's restart also gave Lane the vantage point to see, right up close, how the two leaders each behaved on the restart. Lane made mental notes of everything he sensed about that restart. The two leaders might not repeat their restart tactics again in the event of a late-race caution. But then again, they might.

The long final stage soon became more of a race of attrition than a race of skill and car setup. With the track rubbered up all the way to the top, cars nearly all moved up near the wall, where Darlington tended to offer its greatest speed. But some drivers are better wall runners than others. Car after car began to tag the wall.

Darlington's white outside retaining wall soon began to bear its telltale long black streaks, where cars had rubbed their paint schemes in perilous taps, slides, and skids into the wall. Cars began sporting blurred paint schemes on their right sides, scrubbed into streaks by Darlington's outside wall. Many cars sported the notorious Darlington stripe, a rite of passage among the track's newer drivers.

Lane's car, though, bore no stripe. Lane was among the fewer, more-talented drivers who appeared to have a knack for wall running. He hadn't raced Darlington enough yet at the Cup level to cement his wall-runner reputation. But he was on his way toward that elevated status.

Despite the constant brushes with its wall, Darlington did not produce a grand wreck. Drivers pressed on toward the race's end. With twenty laps to go, though, two cars wrecked after one collided so sharply with the wall as to slide back down across the track in the other car's path.

The caution brought pit strategy to the fore. Lane, the two leaders ahead of him, and the several cars behind him all pitted for four tires. Darlington's abrasive track demanded as much. But a few cars further back took just two right-side tires. And a handful of cars way back in the pack, Darnell included, gambled on skipping the pit stop entirely.

When the race restarted, Lane and the two pitting leaders ahead of him found themselves in the third and fourth rows, behind the cars that had not pitted or had taken just two tires.

Elena and Dani atop Lane's pit box, and the huge crowd in the grandstand, stood for the restart. The restart succeeded, avoiding the common race-end wrecks. Lane and the two other cars just ahead of him with four fresh tires began picking off the cars with older tires, one by one.

With just five laps to go, Lane and the other two cars ahead of him with four fresh tires passed Darnell. Dani groaned beside Elena, atop Lane's pit box. Elena gave Dani a quick comforting hug.

Just then, though, another car further back in the pack broke loose from low on the turn, crashing up into the outside wall. The yellow caution flew once again, bringing the field to a crawl behind the pace car.

Track cleanup took just long enough to bring the race to the point of ending with a green-white- checkered finish. The restart under green would mean just two laps to go. The next time across the start/finish line would mean one lap to go, with the checkered coming the next time around.

No one pitted. Lane, just behind the two leaders, once again chose the outside lane for the restart. Lane and the two leaders in the front row ahead of him would thus restart in the same configuration they had earlier in the race, when Lane had pushed the leader ahead, while taking note of both leaders' restart tactics.

Darnell would restart right behind Lane in the third row.

The crowd stood, the pace car pulled down pit road, and the leaders leapt forward as their cars entered the restart zone.

Lane once again pushed the car ahead of him sharply forward, although more so than the prior restart. Indeed, Lane pushed so aggressively that both the leader ahead of him and Lane's own car cleared the car on the inside lane, which had failed to launch with the same timing.

As soon as both cars were clear, Lane pulled down into the inside lane beneath and alongside the leader. Just at that point, though, the car ahead of which Lane pulled had gained its momentum. That car pushed Lane ahead of the leader on the outside lane. As soon as Lane cleared the car on the outside, he pulled up in front of it. Lane now led the race on the outside, exactly as he planned.

By this time, the leaders had just reached and passed under the white flag. One lap remained. Lane had only to hold the lead, and he would win the race.

Darnell, meanwhile, had been the beneficiary of his own back-and-forth pushing on the restart. Darnell remained close behind the three leaders ahead of him. If those three leaders bumped one another, tagged the wall, or otherwise stumbled, Darnell might just win.

And that's when the remarkable happened.

Darnell had no plan other than to patiently wait for any opening around the last lap. His car had older tires and had no chance of catching the leaders, including Lane, unless the leaders wrecked or otherwise seriously stumbled. But Darnell's car, already riding up along the wall like the other leaders, suddenly leapt forward down the last of the back straightaway and into the final great curve at the tight end of Darlington's oval.

To the limited extent that Darnell could think at all, under the remarkable strain of the event, he thought briefly of the engine control module. But by the time his car hit the curve, it was already hard up against the wall. Darnell was riding the wall around the last turn, just like the famous *Hail Melon*.

Fortunately, Lane had pulled off the wall toward the inside of the track after negotiating the very last turn, heading toward the finish line. Lane had done so to block the two cars right behind him. That path left an opening for Darnell's car to shoot around the last turn, carrying its full-speed momentum down the home straightaway, past Lane and the other two cars behind him.

Darnell's car flashed under the checkered flag in first place, followed closely by Lane in second. The two other cars finished right behind Lane.

The extraordinary finish produced a sort of bedlam. Fans were excited and aghast. Commentators quickly drew the *Hail Melon* parallel, noting that the maneuver was illegal. They correctly reported, swiftly confirmed by race officials, that the maneuver would disqualify Darnell, placing him last.

For his part, Darnell had to quickly explain what had happened, or the entire community might assume that he was as foolish as his buoyant personality sometimes suggested. Darnell did so, immediately over his race radio and in a pit road interview shortly after the race, by pointing to his car's faulty engine control module. Darnell hadn't floored the accelerator into the wall at all. He had just ridden the out-of-control car across the finish line, only to limp back to pit road effectively destroyed.

In sharing his account, Darnell made no mention of any conspiracy. Rob had coached Darnell that only the stock-car association and its security and public-relations team would make any such disclosure, if such a disclosure would ever be forthcoming. Darnell simply attributed it to an equipment failure.

That isn't to say that Darnell didn't enjoy the notoriety. To the contrary, consistent with his comedic personality, Darnell played up the event to its hilt. In his post-race interview, Darnell gleamed with the excitement of his wild ride, calling it an involuntary but nonetheless priceless *Hail Melon*. Darnell professed to have enjoyed every exhilarating second of his wild ride, even if he claimed nothing to do with it.

It was likewise immediately evident to everyone, when race officials confirmed it with the field still circling the track back to pit road, that Lane had won the race.

Lane's crew chief promptly radioed Lane with that confirmation.

"You're the winner, Big Guy," the crew chief called.

"Everyone else alright?" Lane asked, thinking of Darnell and his wild ride.

"All good," Billy replied from the spotters stand high above, adding, "Just checked. Darnell's shaken but all smiles."

As the field pulled down pit road, Lane remained on the track for the celebratory burnout. Pulling the smoking car up to the flag stand, Lane climbed out of the car for the on-track interview. The interviewer congratulated Lane, letting him share his thanks for the win and his immediate impressions. The interviewer then asked Lane about Darnell's wild wall ride.

"I just hope the fans enjoyed it," Lane said to an appreciative roar from the crowd, adding, "Because we'll probably never see it again."

19

Lane brought his car around to pit road and victory lane, after his on-track interview concluded. Elena, Dani, Darnell, Blake, Diana, and Marla met Lane there. They watched as Lane celebrated with his crew. One by one, they joined Lane for victory lane photographs, Elena first, then joined by Blake, Diana, and Dani, and eventually joined by Darnell and Marla.

This time, photographers caught the poignant moment over which later generations would marvel, after photographers had missed the several other timeless moments Darlington race week had offered Lane and his family.

The victory lane photograph, with the winner Lane supported by his famous father, beautiful mother and sister, elegant girlfriend, aunt, and sister's boyfriend, would tell stories of love and intertwining family relationships to race fans marveling over the photograph decades later.

The victory lane photograph omitted only one significant family member. Marla's husband Rob was busy advancing and wrapping up a successful security investigation.

Rob's digital forensics and cyber security team had indeed monitored, tracked, and traced the council's race interference, in exactly the way that they had suspected. Armed with substantial evidence of that interference already, the team had been able, during the Darlington race, to pinpoint the responsible devices and methods. They had also been able to trace the actions to the council.

Rob, though, had one last investigative action to execute, before word reached the council that his team had cracked their interference.

"Ready for a shower and change at the motorhome?" Rob called from the shadows to Lane, as Lane sat exhausted on the victory lane platform.

Lane looked up at Rob with a weary smile, nodding. Excusing himself from the last remaining celebrating crew members, Lane ambled sorely off toward the motorhome. Rob walked beside him.

As they approached the motorhome, they both noticed the telltale white sedan parked alongside it. When they reached the motorhome's door, though, no one emerged from the white sedan. Rob and Lane had both expected to see Doyle.

Rob and Lane paused at the motorhome's door, waiting. Soon, several shadowy figures emerged from the surrounding darkness. They encircled the sedan.

Rob shrugged, saying to Lane, "Go ahead inside."

Lane dutifully opened the motorhome door to slowly mount the steps inside. When Lane had closed the motorhome's door behind him, Rob nodded to the circle of shadowy figures. One of them stepped forward, snapping on a bright light to shine through the sedan's tinted windows.

"Out, with your hands up," the chief law-enforcement officer holding the bright light commanded, while motioning to the sedan's occupants.

The sedan's rear door swung open, and three timid, android-like council figures tumbled nervously out, hands dutifully raised. Two other similar figures opened the sedan's front doors to step cautiously out.

"Step away from the vehicle," the chief law-enforcement officer with the light commanded.

The council androids obeyed, huddling up alongside the motorhome. Rob pulled a search warrant from his pocket. Holding it up for the council androids to inspect, Rob explained, "To search you and the vehicle, and seize the vehicle and any devices."

The other law enforcement figures stepped forward out of the shadows to descend on the white sedan. They soon removed tablets, laptop computers, and other electronic paraphernalia. Two of the law-enforcement officers turned aside to search the council androids, reaping a stash of cellphones, smartwatches, and other electronic devices.

The council androids remained silent and compliant throughout the search and seizure. One of the law-enforcement officers pulled a card from his pocket, from which he read the council androids their rights.

As soon as the officer had finished, Rob asked, "Where's Doyle?"

The council androids looked at one another with blank stares and shrugs. One of them turned to Rob, saying, "Who's Doyle?"

"Your leader," Rob replied, "Your leader who has been in this white sedan outside this motorhome at most every other race."

Once again, the council androids looked at one another with shrugs. The one who had spoken to Rob said again, "We don't have any leader. We follow the algorithm."

"Then why are you here, outside this motorhome?" Rob asked.

"The algorithm told us to be here," came the answer.

Rob pulled a business card from his pocket. Handing it to the council android who had spoken, Rob said, "Your legal representatives are to meet us tomorrow at noon at this office address."

The android looked at the card, then at Rob, then at the other council androids, and then finally nodded to Rob.

Rob turned to the law-enforcement officer who had read the council androids their rights. That officer said to the androids, "You're free to go."

The sedan's android driver stepped forward with its keys, preparing to re-enter the sedan. The officer, though, stepped in front of the android, holding out his hand for the keys while saying, "The sedan stays with us."

The driver android slowly handed the officer the keys. The council androids all looked at one another. The driver android then led them slowly off.

The council's legal and corporate representatives appeared at the motorsport's corporate offices right on time the next day. An assistant showed them into a boardroom with a large conference table in the middle. The council's representatives sat on one side, and the motorsport's representatives on the other side. A large video screen glowed behind the head of the conference table, ready for its presentation.

Rob, Dani, and members of their digital security team then spent the first two hours methodically laying out the evidence they had acquired of the council's match fixing, attempted bribery, attempted extortion, violations of state and federal electronic records, wiretapping, and surveillance acts, and attempted murder. Rob deliberately had no state or federal officials present, only the evidence their authorizations had helped Rob's team acquire.

The sides then took a break for private caucuses. When they reconvened, the council's chief legal representative asked what the motorsport was demanding to resolve all issues without criminal charges.

Sliding a draft settlement agreement across the large conference table, Rob began listing the conditions one by one. They included the council's prompt abolition, the council's return or destruction of all records, files, and other electronic information the council had acquired during the brief course of its contractual relationship with the motorsport, and a confidentiality clause with respect to anything any council member or employee had learned, in any way related to the motorsport or its employees, drivers, teams, officials, or fans.

Technical employees of the council would fully cooperate with the motorsport's follow-on data provider to ensure a smooth transition of data operations. Finally, the council would refund all fees the motorsport paid and disgorge all associated profits, into a fund the motorsport would establish, own, and operate for the care of retired indigent drivers, pit crew members, mechanics, and others associated with the sport.

"Oh, and one more thing," Rob added as he concluded the long list of conditions, "The council must disclose the identity, address, other contact information, title, role, and activities of this Doyle figure."

"We know nothing of this Doyle figure," the council's chief legal representative immediately replied, adding, "But we will agree to divulge any information about him that we may in the future discover."

"And that's what the agreement in front of you so provides," Rob replied, pointing to the lengthy document he had slid across the table in front of the chief legal representative.

Without reading a word of the document, the chief legal representative flipped it open to its last, signature page, pulled a gilded pen from his inside suit-coat breast pocket, and signed the document with a flourish. Without another glance at it, he slid it back across the table to Rob.

Rob didn't move, didn't change expression, didn't look at or touch the document, and instead just stared back at the chief legal representative. The chief legal representative rose. His team spread up and down his side of the conference table rose with him. And they marched silently out in a defeated procession.

Rob turned to Dani seated beside him, saying, "Welcome to the security team."

Dani smiled, saying, "I like this work. I think it's going to be rewarding, satisfying, and exciting."

Rob smiled back, saying, "You and Darnell make quite a pair."

20

"Hop in," Lane said to Elena after he reached across the empty passenger seat to fling open his car's passenger door.

Elena stooped outside the passenger side of the car to peer in at Lane. She said, "I don't know. My momma taught me never to ride with strangers."

Lane laughed. Elena joined in the laughter as she hopped in beside Lane. Lane began to back the car out of Rob and Marla's drive.

"Where are we going?" Elena asked with relish.

"Big secret," Lane replied playfully.

"Then just tell me if I'm dressed appropriately," Elena answered.

"Gorgeous," Lane replied.

"No, no," Elena objected, adding, "I didn't ask if I looked alright. If we're hiking or canoeing or hunting or something, then I'll need to change."

"No, none of those things," Lane replied, adding, "You're dressed fine. You'll be comfortable."

"Darn," Elena replied with her own playfulness, adding, "I was hoping you'd make me uncomfortable."

"I can try," Lane joked back.

"You do that," Elena retorted with a mischievous smile.

They were already out on the highway, headed farther out from town and into the beautiful, rolling countryside.

"Are you hungry?" Lane asked.

"No," Elena replied, adding, "But let's stop for coffee if we've got a bit of a drive ahead of us."

Lane nodded. He turned down the shortest route to their favorite coffee shop. Pulling in the coffee shop's parking lot, Lane offered, "Wait right here. I'll be right back."

Lane soon reappeared with their favorite breakfast drinks and muffins.

"Yum," Elena said as Lane handed the muffins over while climbing back in the car.

They chatted, drank coffee, and snacked happily on muffins as they drove further out into the country. Elena kept breaking off bits of muffin to feed Lane as Lane drove. Elena laughed each time, pretending that Lane was her infant boy. Lane laughed with her.

Soon, they slowed along the highway, turning down a seldom-driven country lane.

"I hope you know where you're going," Elena said as they proceeded down the little-used lane. She added, "Because I still have no clue what you're up to, and I'm pretty hard to fool."

Lane glanced over at Elena. The whole trip he had been waiting for a signal, an answer, a hint. He could at any moment turn aside, alter his plans and mission. He had deliberately left things uncertain enough, open enough, that he could turn back at a moment's notice, and Elena would never know of his conditional plan.

But as Lane glanced at Elena again, her lively eyes, playful voice, and delightful laughter resonated through his soul. And as they did so, Lane felt more and more assured of his conditional plan, more ready to proceed with this next adventure.

Lane slowed the car as they came upon a private drive off the little-used road. He turned the car down the private drive.

"I don't know," Elena said, adding, "It said *private drive*. I hope you have the owner's permission."

Lane smiled a broad smile, saying, "Oh, I do. I do."

As they wended their way further down the drive, past beautiful fields, woods, and ponds, a charming new home came into view, just up a hill from a larger pond. Sunlight reflected off the home's sparkling windows and shimmered on the surface of the pond.

"Enchanting," Elena said in a soft voice, adding, "Imagine living here. You've got some very fortunate friends."

Lane smiled, repeating only, "Imagine living here. What would that be like?"

Lane stopped the car a short distance from the gleaming new home. He turned off the car. Looking at Elena, he said again, "Imagine living here. What would that be like?"

Tears began to form in Elena's eyes. She shook her head, saying, "Lane, don't you play tricks on me. I'll never forgive you if you do."

"I'm not playing a trick on you," Lane assured Elena, taking her hand.

Tears began streaming down Elena's cheeks, as she continued to shake her head in disbelief.

"This home and land is ours," Lane said, "If you wish to live here, husband and wife, with me."

Now sobbing happy tears, Elena asked, "Was that a marriage proposal?"

Lane nodded, saying simply, "Yes."

"I accept," Elena replied between sobs. As she did so, she bent across the car's console to bury her head in Lane's shoulder.

Darlington Dawn

www.ingramcontent.com/pod-product-compliance
Lightning Source LLC
LaVergne TN
LVHW031606060526
838201LV00063B/4746